Cambridge Topics in English Language

Language and Gender

Felicity Titjen
Series Editors: Dan Clayton and Marcello Giovanelli

CAMBRIDGE
UNIVERSITY PRESS

University Printing House, Cambridge CB2 8BS, United Kingdom

One Liberty Plaza, 20th Floor, New York, NY 10006, USA

477 Williamstown Road, Port Melbourne, VIC 3207, Australia

4843/24, 2nd Floor, Ansari Road, Daryaganj, Delhi – 110002, India

79 Anson Road, #06–04/06, Singapore 079906

Cambridge University Press is part of the University of Cambridge.

It furthers the University's mission by disseminating knowledge in the pursuit of education, learning and research at the highest international levels of excellence.

www.cambridge.org
Information on this title: www.cambridge.org/9781108402170

© Cambridge University Press 2018

This publication is in copyright. Subject to statutory exception and to the provisions of relevant collective licensing agreements, no reproduction of any part may take place without the written permission of Cambridge University Press.

First published 2018

20 19 18 17 16 15 14 13 12 11 10 9 8 7 6 5 4 3 2 1

Printed in Malaysia by Vivar Printing

A catalogue record for this publication is available from the British Library

ISBN 978-1-108-40217-0 Paperback

Cambridge University Press has no responsibility for the persistence or accuracy of URLs for external or third-party internet websites referred to in this publication, and does not guarantee that any content on such websites is, or will remain, accurate or appropriate.

....

NOTICE TO TEACHERS IN THE UK

It is illegal to reproduce any part of this work in material form (including photocopying and electronic storage) except under the following circumstances:
(i) where you are abiding by a licence granted to your school or institution by the Copyright Licensing Agency;
(ii) where no such licence exists, or where you wish to exceed the terms of a licence, and you have gained the written permission of Cambridge University Press;
(iii) where you are allowed to reproduce without permission under the provisions of Chapter 3 of the Copyright, Designs and Patents Act 1988, which covers, for example, the reproduction of short passages within certain types of educational anthology and reproduction for the purposes of setting examination questions.

Contents

Series introduction vi
How to use this book vii
Topic introduction viii

1. Historical perspectives 1
   1.1 Introduction: the gender debate 2
   1.2 The 'deficit' approach 4
   1.3 The variationist approach to gender study 7
   1.4 The 'dominance' approach 9
   1.5 The 'difference' approach 10
   1.6 The 'diversity' approach 11
   1.7 Gendered language: censorship or correction? 13
   1.8 The 'performance' approach 14
   1.9 Recognising and celebrating diverse identities 16
   1.10 Conclusion 17

2. Language and gender 18
   2.1 Introduction 19
   2.2 Defining gender: it's all in the name 19
   2.3 Male firstness: word order and generic terms 21
   2.4 Marking gender 23
   2.5 Patterns and metaphors 28
   2.6 Cleaning up language 33
   2.7 Conclusion 36

3. Gender and representation — 37

   3.1 Introduction — 38

   3.2 Exploring gender and discourse — 38

   3.3 Semiotics: Signs and gender — 39

   3.4 Representing gender through metaphor — 43

   3.5 Gender and power — 44

   3.6 Gender and social actor representation — 46

   3.7 Different discourses about gender — 51

   3.8 Gender representation in the media: health magazines — 52

   3.9 Gender and argumentation theory — 53

   3.10 Gender representation in corpus data: talking and writing about sportspeople — 56

   3.11 Conclusion — 58

4. Gender and identity — 60

   4.1 Introduction — 61

   4.2 Identity in discourse: socially constructed selves in private talk — 62

   4.3 Exploring identity and masculinities — 64

   4.4 Identity and constructing selves through phonological choices — 67

   4.5 Occupational talk: conveying a gendered identity in the workplace — 69

   4.6 Social constructing self: performing gender in public and written contexts — 72

   4.7 Performing and constructing gender identity in a modern world — 74

   4.8 Conclusion — 76

5. Exploring gender: applying research methods to data — 77

   5.1 Introduction — 78

   5.2 Creating your own research project — 79

   5.3 Finding spoken data — 88

   5.4 Analysing conversations and making transcripts — 89

   5.5 Reading about language and gender — 93

   5.6 Acknowledging your sources — 94

   5.7 Practising decision-making — 95

   5.8 Conclusion — 97

Ideas and answers — 98

Transcription key — 105

References — 106

Glossary — 108

Index — 113

Acknowledgments — 114

Series introduction

Cambridge Topics in English Language is a series of accessible introductory study guides to major scholarly topics in the fields of English language and linguistics. These books have been designed for use by students at advanced level and beyond and provide detailed overviews of each topic together with the latest research in the field so as to provide a clear introduction that is both practical and up to date.

In all of the books in this series, we have drawn on examples of spoken and written language. We hope these will encourage you to apply the theories, concepts and methods that you will learn in the books to analyse data and to think critically about a number of issues and debates relating to language in use. Many of the books also draw on data from the Cambridge Corpus. Throughout each book, you will find short activities to help develop reading and writing skills, longer extended activities and practice questions that will enable you to explore your learning in more detail and research findings that will provide inspiration for your own language investigations. Each of the chapters includes suggested wider reading, and a full glossary and reference section at the end of each book will support you to extend your learning and provide avenues for future reading and research.

We hope that each book will give you a good overview of its topic and, that taken as a whole, the series will map out some of the most interesting and diverse areas of language study, providing you with fresh thinking and new ideas as you embark on your studies.

Dan Clayton

Marcello Giovanelli

How to use this book

Throughout this book you will notice recurring features that are designed to help your learning. Here is a brief overview of what you'll find.

> **Coverage list**
> A short list of what you will learn in each chapter.

> **KEY TERM**
> Definitions of important terms to help your understanding of the topic.

> **ACTIVITY**
> A clearly defined task to help you apply what you've learnt.

> **RESEARCH QUESTION**
> A longer task to help you go deeper into the topic.

> **PRACTICE QUESTION**
> To give you some practice of questions you might encounter in the exam.

Ideas and answers
Further information, suggestions and answers to all activities and practice questions in the book.

Wider reading
Key texts to help extend your learning.

Topic introduction

A whole book on the topic of gender suggests it's an important issue for linguistics. Indeed, it's still a hotly debated topic by academics in universities around the world.

But is it just a language issue? Arguably, it's as much a *social* issue. The language that we use about men and women, as well as the language used by speakers of different genders, says much about what we think, as a society, about issues of gender and identity.

In this book, my aim is to give you both a little of the history of gender study and the major theories about it. I want to show you how the changing and updating of arguments have reflected society's changing attitudes to gender and identity over the last century. Yet the book is not simply about the past. It's about the present day too. English, as a language, hasn't stayed still. We've transformed and adapted it – through our words and their meanings, as well as in some of our grammar – to represent different views and beliefs about gender. So I want to show you that the English language itself is a vital, dynamic force in understanding gender.*

Even from this introduction, you might already be forming questions about language and gender:

- Isn't gender just a matter of biology?

- Is gender the most important aspect of our identity?

- Does the way we speak about men and women really matter?

I really encourage you to keep questioning as you read. This book offers different interpretations of gender and language so that you can make active choices about further investigations into the area.

From my own experience, I know how enjoyable a topic gender is for both learning and teaching. I hope you'll find this too. Remember, it's also a topic that we can't escape from in our daily lives – it's everywhere around us in our media (and social media) dominated world. But that's what gives it relevance to us all – we help shape it as we interact with each other and perhaps gender shapes us too.

*There is a transcription key at the end of the book to help you in your reflections.

Felicity Titjen

Chapter 1
Historical perspectives

In this chapter you will:

- Explore how approaches to language and gender study have changed over time
- Be introduced to the different perspectives taken to gender by linguists
- Begin to understand how the different perspectives on gender can influence our interpretation of the language used by women and men

1 Language and Gender

1.1 Introduction: the gender debate

In the twentieth century, linguists began to become interested in gender as a language *variable*. In particular, they were fascinated by whether men and women used language in different ways. Of course, today, more recent scrutiny of what 'gender' actually means has reignited the debate again.

Three Ds mark the twentieth-century gender debate – *deficit*, *dominance* and *difference*. What they have in common is that they all define and judge women's language against that used by men, something that we'll be exploring in more detail through this chapter. However, more recently, the focus has shifted to how society influences the language we use and whether we actually 'perform' our gender by demonstrating features and ways of speaking associated with being a woman or a man. These debates have altered as society and its attitudes have changed, with movements such as feminism and changing attitudes towards equality affecting not only gender but sexuality, disability, and race, amongst others.

> **KEY TERMS**
>
> **Variable:** a contextual factor that can influence speech and writing
>
> **Deficit theory:** the belief that the language used by women is inferior to that used by men
>
> **Dominance theory of language:** the belief that the language differences between men and women can be explained by the hierarchical dominance of men in society
>
> **Difference theory of language:** the belief that men and women have innate differences in the style and function of their speech and writing

Before we start exploring the various approaches taken to explaining gender and language use, we need to try to define the concept of gender itself.
This is important as it informs our collective ways of thinking about gender. Firstly, gender can be identified as a biologically determined difference: we are born either male or female. Secondly, we can think of it as a socially shaped difference from birth, through such things as dress, toys and the language used to present gender to us.

Historical perspectives

RESEARCH QUESTION
Feminism and women's rights

The history of language and gender study is also linked to the social and political history of feminism and changing attitudes to women, especially in the twentieth century. It's therefore a good idea for you to start by gaining a broader understanding of the social, historical and political contexts. Research these topic areas (either individually or in groups):

- a chronological summary of these movements: first-wave feminism, second-wave feminism and post-modern feminism
- legal changes to women's rights (political, employment, sexual)
- social changes (work, occupation and domestic roles)

You could present your findings in a slide format or simply make your own notes.

KEY TERMS

First-wave feminism: the movement that focused on getting the right for women to vote, to have property rights and the right to an education

Second-wave feminism: the movement that focused on women's roles and rights within the workplace and in reproductive, sexuality and family issues

Post-modern feminism: the movement that covers different views and beliefs about women's rights and sees women as individuals as well as part of a group

1 Language and Gender

1.2 The 'deficit' approach

In this approach, male language is seen as the norm and women's language is viewed as deficient to men's. This was the view of the earliest researchers into gender, based on:

1 Identifying women's language as different to that of men
2 Judging women's language as inferior.

1.2.1 Otto Jespersen and an early study into women's language

In 1922, Danish linguist Otto Jespersen published *Language: Its nature, Development and Origin*. This included a chapter titled 'The Woman' where he explored some of his ideas about women's language – interestingly, there was no corresponding chapter for men, showing his view that perhaps men's language was the norm and so did not need special discussion. Jespersen offered observations about women's conversational strategies, arguing that women much more often than men break off without finishing their sentences, because they start talking without having thought out what they are going to say.

He also argued that women's language could simply be typified as 'lively chatter' since their roles consisted of:

> 'the care of the children, cooking, brewing, baking, sewing, washing etc, things that for the most part demanded no deep thought'. (Jespersen 1922)

One of the criticisms of Jespersen's work was that it was observational, and not based on detailed evidence. Yet it could be argued that one positive from his ideas was that gender was being investigated and emphasis was being placed on women as worthy of linguistic study. Jespersen was undertaking a form of ethnographic research (something that we'll be looking at later in Chapter 5 as a research method), as he was basing his findings on participant observation and in natural settings, and this allowed him to see language use in practice. But Jespersen's work is what would be called folk linguistics today, meaning that many of his points represent basic and flawed ideas about women's language that seem more anecdotal than based on valid and reliable research methods.

Historical perspectives

> **KEY TERMS**
>
> **Ethnographic research:** the systematic study of groups of people and cultures carried out by close observation
>
> **Folk linguistics:** the opinions and beliefs that non-linguists hold about language use

ACTIVITY 1.1
Exploring folk linguistics

To test out some common perceptions in folk linguistics, ask family and friends what they think about the following statements:

- Women talk more than men.
- Women gossip more than men.
- Women ask more questions than men.
- Women are better listeners than men.
- Women will talk about anything but men are more economical with words.

Keeping a record of their responses will introduce you to some of the strategies that you can use to generate data when investigating a particular language topic. (We are going to explore this in more detail in Chapter 5, along with the ethical considerations that you need to be mindful of.) Here are some options:

- You could ask people to write down their own responses.
- You could record them (with their permission, of course) and transcribe their responses.
- Finally, you could interview them and note down their responses yourself.
- Whatever method you use, collate their responses and see if there is a pattern in the beliefs expressed. There might be some overall similarities or, if you have obtained information on the age and gender of the respondents, you might be able to identify some differences. You should also consider the evidence that your respondents offer for these beliefs. What anecdotal evidence do they offer for believing that these are 'truthful' statements?

1 Language and Gender

1.2.2 Robin Lakoff and women's language

The observational approach started by Jespersen continued with the next wave of linguistic focus on gender, and specifically women's language, with Robin Lakoff's *Language and Woman's Place* published in 1975. Lakoff made it clear that she was looking at a very specific group of women – American, white, middle class and educated – but her findings were interpreted as relating to all women.

Lakoff labelled women's spoken language in a way that implied an almost complete dissimilarity from men's language, and characterised it as having linguistic features that highlighted women's uncertainty and powerlessness. Even the linguistic labels Lakoff used appeared to confirm that women's language was inferior to men's. For example, she claimed that women used 'empty' adjectives, a questioning intonation on statements and hedges in their spoken interactions. These lexical and prosodic choices are all seen, to an extent, as undermining the content of the talk and foregrounding women's lack of authority.

ACTIVITY 1.2
Revisiting Lakoff's colour study

You can use one of Lakoff's findings to conduct an experiment, testing her interesting assumption that men and women have different lexicons. Lakoff concluded that women had a much more extensive and subtle vocabulary for colours than men. She deduced that whereas men might identify a colour shade as simply blue, purple or green, women were likely to make finer distinctions. To exemplify this, according to Lakoff when asking a woman to label something that is purple in colour, women might label particular shades as 'lavender', 'lilac', 'mauve', 'violet' or 'indigo'.

- Take a colour chart and cut out some of the range of options for the colours blue, green and purple.

- Ask five males and five females to describe the colour they can see. Either speak to each participant separately so that they cannot influence each other, or photocopy the colours onto a sheet of paper and ask them to write down the colour term that they would use to describe this beneath each one.

Can you find any evidence to support Lakoff's claims? Do you think that any other factors apart from gender might impact the kind of responses you got? (Lakoff suggested that sexuality might also impact the use of special lexicon, as her notion of men's colour identification was based on a heterosexual male.)

1.3 The variationist approach to gender study

One of Lakoff's claims was that in addition to being politer than men, women also used more standard forms of English. This was not new. Other well-known earlier studies by variational sociolinguists had found this pattern, most notably those undertaken by William Labov and Peter Trudgill. Interest in sociolinguistic variations evolved out of the study of dialectology rather than an interest in gender and combined some significant factors:

- A focus on how language varies and changes in particular communities of speakers
- Recognition that other social factors were relevant (age, gender and how much part of the community people were)
- An exploration of linguistic structures (such as phonology and grammar).

    Labov's emphasis was on using reliable and ethical data generation methods – valuing these above just personal intuition – and creating corpora of speech recordings from a wide range of speakers that made his findings more valid.

KEY TERMS

Variational sociolinguistics: the study of the way that language changes in communities of speakers and the interaction between social factors and linguistic features

Dialectology: the study of accents and dialects

Corpora: a large collection of data usually stored electronically

One of his most famous studies was that of New York Department Stores (Labov 1966). In this he asked shop assistants in three different stores – Saks Fifth Avenue (an upmarket and expensive store), Macy's (a mid-priced store) and S. Klein (a cheap store) – the same questions in order to get them to say a particular sound – an 'r' sound in 'fourth floor'. Labov was investigating the 'r' sound that appears after a vowel (as in 'car') that New Yorkers would associate with a higher class of speaker. Although his studies were not primarily focused on women's language use, he concluded, like Lakoff, that women (of all social classes) are more likely to use the perceived correct term or the pronunciation with more social status attached to it. He also found that women often use hypercorrection (the over application of a perceived grammatical rule, for

Language and Gender

example saying 'between you and I' instead of 'between you and me') and believed that women used this in order to gain what he named overt prestige, or respect from others for using the correct form.

In his 1972 investigation, Trudgill explored whether people from Norwich, a city in the East of England, pronounced the *-ing* suffix on verbs like 'walking' and 'going' (Trudgill 1972). His findings showed a marked difference between men's and women's use of the more 'correct' Standard English form. As women used the standard form more frequently in formal situations, despite using the non-standard form in their casual speech, he concluded that women saw the standard form as a way of signalling or gaining social status and, consequently, prestige. In his later work, Labov (2001: 293) coined the term gender paradox to describe how women prefer to use forms of language that seem to have more prestige, but stated that women also tend more than men to use creative, newer forms of language.

> ### KEY TERMS
>
> **Hypercorrection:** a pronunciation, word form or grammatical construction mistakenly perceived to be standard usage and substituted in a desire to be correct
>
> **Overt prestige:** status gained by speakers from using a particular dialect or language
>
> **Standard English:** a dialect of English considered 'correct' and 'normal', because it has distinctive and standardised features of spelling, vocabulary and syntax; it is the form of English usually used in formal writing
>
> **Gender paradox:** the phenomenon that women use more prestigious standard forms of English than men but that they also lead language change by adopting new forms of everyday English

ACTIVITY 1.3
Testing men's and women's use of standard and non-standard forms

Both Labov's and Trudgill's research explored how sounds were produced by different speakers and the variables that affected these (class, age, gender, etc.). As you saw, Trudgill focused particularly on the pronunciation of the suffix *-ing*.

You can also investigate whether women and men seem to say *-ing* differently, either by pronouncing it with the 'g' or by omitting it and

Historical perspectives

ending the word with 'n' (so it sounds more like *goin'*). Here are two research options for you:

- Use an internet search engine to find song lyrics by solo female and solo male artists. Highlight all the words that end in the 'n' sound. Listen to recordings of these songs and identify where the singers use the 'g' sound or end the word with the 'n' sound. Can you find a difference between the male and the female singers?

- Write a list of five words ending with the *-ing* suffix or a paragraph containing these. Ask women and men to read these out and record their responses, after you have their permission. Tally by gender the speakers who pronounce the 'g' or end with the 'n'. Is there any difference between the genders?

1.4 The 'dominance' approach

The dominance approach occurred against the historical and political backdrop of second-wave feminism, which had a central goal of removing gender inequality. This approach understands men as positioned above women because of their social and political power. From a language perspective, men were seen as using language as a means of reinforcing or maintaining their power in conversations, and women were viewed as asserting their lack of power through their language choices.

1.4.1 Testing the dominance approach

Numerous further studies in the 1970s and 1980s seemed to confirm Lakoff's ideas. Many researchers focused on recording same-sex and mixed-sex conversations, identifying dominance from the features Lakoff had already identified or finding other ones. One of the most famous of these was Don Zimmerman's and Candace West's (1975) college campus study, which found that men were responsible for 96 per cent of the interruptions in conversations occurring between men and women. Men's dominance seems from these to lie in their conversational management – i.e. speaking more, having longer turns and, in conversations with women, being interrupted less and interrupting more.

Dale Spender, in *Man Made Language* (1980), drew further attention to this verbal dominance by interpreting women's silence as a form of oppression. However, linguists also saw other types of language as asserting dominance, although perhaps more subtle than men interrupting women in conversation. Just as Lakoff saw asymmetry used in labels for men and women (for example, 'master'/'mistress'), Spender saw language as asserting male dominance in the

Language and Gender

generic use of the male pronoun 'he' and the ultimate dominance of having an all-powerful God as male.

> **KEY TERM**
>
> **Asymmetry:** a power imbalance between speakers shown by the unequal way they address each other

Pamela Fishman, in her 1980 study of conversations between three American couples, drew similar conclusions to Lakoff. Fishman viewed the hard 'work' that women do in conversations as the result of their inferior social status – something she had already noted in earlier studies and called 'interactional shitwork' (Fishman 1977: 99–101). This focus on the styles of men and women in talk led to the next approach to studying gender.

1.5 The 'difference' approach

What began to emerge was a debate about whether male dominance was enough of an explanation or if there was indeed a difference between male and female language. What academics now began to debate was what might account for the difference. Was it a simple matter of biology or was it the result of social factors? So, research began to focus on exploring both men's and women's language and looking at their verbal behaviours and even the conversational topics that they chose.

1.5.1 Mars and Venus: the great divide

Deborah Tannen is one of the most influential academics whose work represented the difference view. She argued that male–female conversation could be viewed as a form of miscommunication where women were naturally inclined to be cooperative in conversation, and men more competitive.

Table 1.1: Pairs of differences between men and women

Men	Women
Status	Support
Advice	Understanding
Orders	Proposals
Conflict	Compromise
Independence	Intimacy
Information	Feelings

Historical perspectives

The title of her book, *You Just Don't Understand: Men and Women in Conversation* (Tannen 1990), highlighted this perceived difference through its title. Within it she established 'six contrasts', which was how she labelled pairs of differences between men and women, as shown in Table 1.1.

Tannen coined the term genderlect to describe the different language use of men and women. It's easy to see how these contrasts may have influenced the types of non-academic self-help relationship books that rely on emphasising these ideas of stereotypical differences. One of the most famous of these was John Gray's 1992 book, *Men are From Mars, Women are from Venus*. Gray used the names of different planets with their classical mythology connotations for the gods (Mars, the Roman god of war and Venus, the Roman god of love) to explore stereotypes.

KEY TERM
Genderlect: the particular language used by men and women according to their gender

1.6 The 'diversity' approach

More recently, sociolinguistics has moved away from the 'three Ds' of gender study (deficit, dominance and difference) to acknowledge instead the importance of individual differences amongst men and women, rather than simply pitting the genders against each other. One of the key research focuses has been on how people within groups use language, calling upon social network theory and the concept of communities of practice, and viewing gender as only one element of our identity. Both of these focus on the shared social nature of our interactions and explain how language behaviours can be affected by the groups that we belong to.

KEY TERMS
Social network theory: the study of how people in organisations and groups interact with each other

Communities of practice: a group of people who come together for the purpose of a shared activity

Language and Gender

1.6.1 Gender and social networks

Links to the work of Labov and Trudgill can be seen in more recent studies that apply Lesley Milroy's social network theory (1980). In Milroy's theory, particular informal and formal relationships create what Milroy calls a 'web of ties' (2002: 550). Patterns of language use evolve as linguistic variation characterises the speech behaviour of groups. In 1982, Jenny Cheshire conducted a study into the use of non-standard linguistic forms used by a group of 25 mainly teenage girls and boys in Reading, England. Her participants were users of adventure playgrounds in the area which were regarded as trouble spots by the residents locally, as some of the children were frequent school truants. She was interested in male and female differences but also considered individual differences too.

Similar to earlier studies, Jenny Cheshire found that girls tended more than boys to alter their language to a prestige form when speaking to their teacher (Cheshire 1982). She argued that the key factor in some girls using more non-standard forms was the degree to which they felt affiliated to the local youth subculture of appearing tough. However, some more individual differences emerged. Of the 12 girls, a third did not associate themselves so much with the other girls and criticised their language and behaviours. Cheshire found that this group of 'good' girls used far fewer non-standard forms than the other girls – a striking 26 per cent compared to the 58 average of the rest of the girls.

1.6.2 Gender and communities of practice

Jean Lave's and Etienne Wenger's community of practice (CoP) model (1991) is a means of describing how people come together for a particular purpose to establish ways of doing things and ways of interacting to achieve their shared purpose. Wenger (1998) separates CoP into three crucial areas of mutual engagement, a joint negotiated enterprise and a shared repertoire. From a gender perspective, other researchers such as Penelope Eckert and Sally McConnell-Ginet (1992) took this notion of a CoP to explore how gender is produced and reproduced within these communities. In their discussion not only did they suggest that we all belong to multiple communities of practice but that our gender may also inform which groups we become members of. The CoP examples that they suggested perhaps reflected the time in which they were writing: they saw men as more traditionally being members of a football team and women as members of a dance-based fitness class. They also proposed that participation levels with the CoP might be impacted by the different roles and status given to women and men within the group, offering the military as an example where women's involvement may not be the same as men's.

Historical perspectives

> **KEY TERMS**
>
> **Mutual engagement:** members of a community of practice come together in a common negotiated activity
>
> **Joint negotiated enterprise:** communities of practice share common goals and work together to achieve them
>
> **Shared repertoire:** communities of practice share the same resources to communicate with each other and may have particular ways of doing or speaking

1.7 Gendered language: censorship or correction?

Another approach has been to recognise diversity through the language choices we make and value this through making conscious decisions to adopt a political correctness strategy and avoid sexist or discriminatory language. Deborah Cameron in her book *Verbal Hygiene* (Cameron 1995) coined this phrase to describe the political correctness movement that sought to 'clean up' language. She defended the sometimes criticised practice of using euphemisms for minority groups because she said that it allows people to understand that the language we use can have social consequences. Rather than viewing political correctness as another form of linguistic prescriptivism and censorship, she presented politically correct language as a means to challenge the idea that one group of people has an undisputed right to decree language over any other group.

> **KEY TERMS**
>
> **Political correctness:** refers to the belief that language should not be used in a discriminatory way
>
> **Euphemism:** words or phrases that are substituted for more direct words or phrases in an attempt to make things easier to accept or less embarrassing
>
> **Prescriptivism:** the notion that language should be fixed, prescribing a set standard of rules for language usage, with any shift away from these rules or standards being seen as incorrect

Deborah Cameron also addressed the issues that some aspects of language are sometimes considered preferable to others – whether it's for moral reasons or it just sounds nicer. She also applied 'verbal hygiene' to explain why women's

Language and Gender

move from domestic roles to the workplace from the 1970s onwards caused some problems. There were long-held stereotypes about the desirable feminine qualities of women's speech and the problem in the workplace, she identified was that women's language was seen as too feminine to be taken seriously. She accounted for this by the fact that through the decades and centuries before, women had not been socialised into speaking in public contexts.

Like Jespersen, she devoted a whole chapter to women. In 'The new Pygmalion: verbal hygiene for women' she surveyed some of the advice given to women as to how to be more successful in the workplace. Here, she used the myth of Pygmalion – and its dramatic presentation in George Bernard Shaw's play – to explore the ways that people seek to 'improve' women. (In the play, the main character Professor Higgins, who is a phonetician, bets that he can turn an ordinary London flower girl into a 'lady' by teaching her to speak "properly".) Even her chapter exploring attitudes to grammar deliberately called upon more prescriptive ideas of male firstness in the ordering of titles 'Mr Syntax and Mrs Grundy', something that we'll be exploring more in Chapter 2.

> **KEY TERM**
>
> **Phonetician:** a person who specialises in the study of sounds

1.8 The 'performance' approach

In the 1990s linguists took a different approach to gender study – that of social constructivism – and this has had a profound influence on ways of thinking about gender in contemporary linguistics. A social constructivist approach moves away from issues of inequality and language as a reflection of gender. Instead it sees gender as active, negotiated and sometimes self-positioned. In a sense it is concerned with a big picture, not of power and inequality, but with what is communicated by, to and about men and women, girls and boys; gender, from this viewpoint, is not a fixed identity but an interpreted identity and one that is socially constructed.

> **KEY TERM**
>
> **Social constructivism:** places the importance on social interaction as constructing identity and people coming together to form a shared construction of the world

Historical perspectives

1.8.1 The trouble with gender: performativity and social constructionism

Judith Butler's book *Gender Trouble* (Butler 1990) raises the argument of gender as a performance. She argues that we are constantly engaged in constructing gender. Here, and in her later work, Butler says that gender is something we *do* and is not what we *are*. The initial basis of her argument stemmed from speech act theory. John Austin (1962) and John Searle (1969) had recognised that certain speech acted as performatives as they brought something into being rather than describing something that existed already. In *Bodies That Matter*, Butler cited the statements such as those performed in a marriage service ('I now pronounce you man and wife') and the kind of statements that people make after a child is born (like 'it's a girl/boy') socially construct gender and start the process of a child being aware that it is being categorised as female or male (Butler 1993: 232).

Butler argues that language use is only one element of this. We have already seen from Robin Lakoff's earlier work that certain linguistic features are closely associated with women's language. This means that speakers could adopt specific language features as a kind of resource to perform being a woman, along with other resources such as clothing, ways of walking, and so on. By calling upon these verbal and non-verbal resources, people are performing being a man or being a woman, and this is a key to Butler's concept of performativity. According to Judith Butler, the ways that we present ourselves, and repeat these presentations, *constructs* our gender rather than *reflects* it.

> **KEY TERMS**
>
> **Speech act theory:** the study of how words can be used to carry out actions
>
> **Performatives:** speech acts that explicitly perform an act, usually in a socially conventional situation such as a wedding ceremony, e.g. saying 'I do'.
>
> **Performativity:** the ability to use speech and other communication methods to construct or perform an identity

You can see this shift from the view that language use *reflects* gender to the view that language use *constructs* gender by considering the difference between saying 'I speak like this because I am male or female' to 'I speak like this and because of this I come across as masculine or feminine'. In the first statement, the speaker is explaining that the language that they use is a result of their gender. In contrast, in the second statement the speaker is announcing that their language choices make them appear more masculine or feminine. Butler

Language and Gender

looks at some situations which expressly call upon the 'performer' to adopt and present more stereotypical expressions of masculine and feminine traits. Butler uses the example of a professional drag queen, as the role calls explicitly upon the male performing to adopt or exaggerate 'female' language and physical markers of women's appearance such as dress and make-up. Butler sees these performances as subversive (upsetting a commonly held view of gender) because they query the ultimate belief in a link between biological sex and gender.

1.9 Recognising and celebrating diverse identities

It is interesting that in the context of the twenty-first century 'diversity' debate, Butler relies on a notion of gender as a binary (male/female), heterosexual model. We now live in a world where identity is not presented simply as binary opposites. There are new and evolving gender and sexual 'identity' labels. Additionally, there is the recognition that religious, ethnic and cultural identities may also affect the enacting or presentation of gender, and that even within the masculine and feminine binary, there are diversities within different masculinities and femininities. And, finally, there is the recognition that gendered language patterns and behaviours may be context-driven and localised. Overall, new directions in research have moved the study of gender away from Jespersen's simplistic model of a global difference between all men and all women.

> **RESEARCH QUESTION**
> **Greetings cards**
>
> In any card shop – online or physical – there are cards deliberately aimed at male and female family members (aunt, uncle, etc.), age-related cards (for example, cards for children or key milestone cards), and cards for key events (births, weddings, etc.) or simply gender-related cards that are aimed at men and women separately.
>
> Survey these and look at how these construct ideas about gender.
>
> - What stereotypes are there of men and women?
> - What topics are associated with men and women?
> - How is gender reproduced in these cards through the images and pictures and through the slogans, jokes or sayings?

1.10 Conclusion

This chapter has given you the story of gender studies from the earliest approaches taken to very recent views, charting the changes of perspective and investigation methods. Many of these will be revisited as we consider in more depth specific aspects of gender and language, identity and representation. Additionally, some of the research methods that these linguists have used – observations, quantitative studies and transcriptions amongst them – are ones that we will return to in Chapter 5 to show the range of research methods available to you to carry out your own investigations into language and gender.

Wider reading

You can find out more about the concepts and ideas in this chapter by reading these books:

Butler, J. (2004) *Undoing Gender*. New York: Routledge.

Coates, J. and Cameron. D. (eds) (1988) *Women in their Speech Communities: New Perspectives on Language and Sex*. London: Longman.

Milroy, L. (1987) *Language and Social Networks* (Second edition). Oxford: Blackwell.

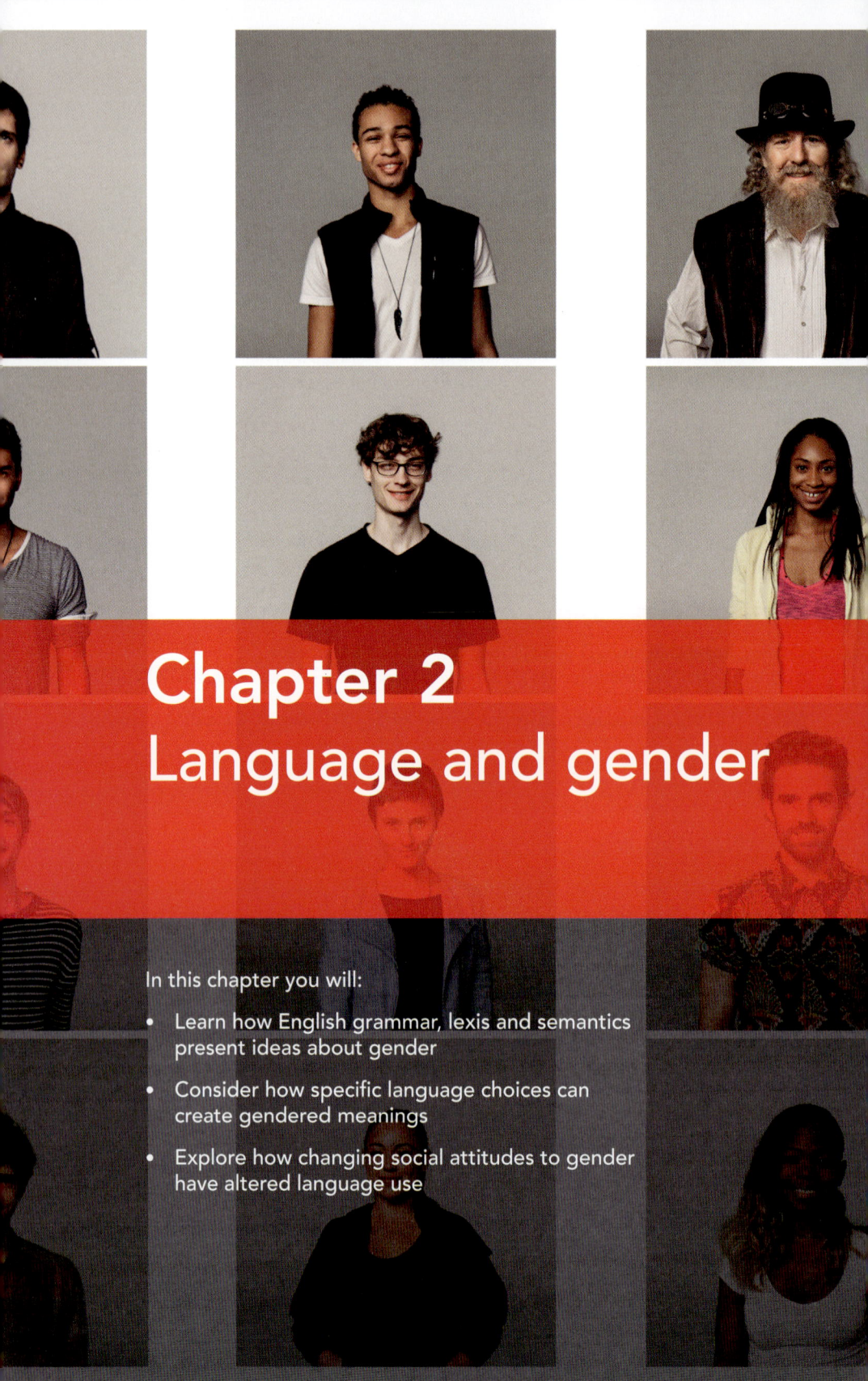

Chapter 2
Language and gender

In this chapter you will:

- Learn how English grammar, lexis and semantics present ideas about gender
- Consider how specific language choices can create gendered meanings
- Explore how changing social attitudes to gender have altered language use

2.1 Introduction

As you saw from Chapter 1, linguists have recently paid greater attention to how language itself can produce and reproduce gender. In this chapter we will explore some of the historical presentations of gender in English lexis and grammar. We will also look at some of the more recent shifts in English usage that have occurred as a result of changing social attitudes both towards women's roles and gender identity. Here our focus is not on modes of communication (for example, speech and writing) but on two significant aspects of gender and language:

- Firstly, that in one major sense, gender can be seen as purely grammatical (gender as the property of a language). Although not true for all languages, in English masculine and feminine gender can be expressed through pronoun choice; the third-person singular 'he' or 'she' expresses two genders.

- Secondly, language is a system that offers speakers and writers choices by which they can present their attitudes to gender. Through their language choices, speakers and writers can present their attitudes to gender.

As you read this chapter, keep in mind two important questions:

1 Does the language we use *influence* social reality and *affect* the way people think about gender?

2 Does the language we use simply *reflect* our society and *mirror* the way people think about gender?

2.2 Defining gender: it's all in the name

A good place to start considering how we view gender is with dictionary definitions. A useful way to start you thinking about some of the issues raised earlier about gender bias and inequality in language is to undertake a simple search of online definitions of man and woman. Look at Table 2.1, which shows definitions and examples of language use for the nouns *man* and *woman* from the Cambridge Dictionary.

2 Language and Gender

Table 2.1: Cambridge Dictionary (online) definitions for 'man' and 'woman'

	Man	Woman
1	an adult male human being *The men's champion in the 400 metres* *Steve can solve anything – the man's a genius.*	an adult female human being *She's a really nice woman.*
2	a male employee	a wife or female sexual partner *Apparently, Jeff has a new woman.*
3	military members of the armed forces who are not officers	women in general
4	a male servant	used to form nouns describing certain types of women or women with certain jobs *Englishwoman, chairwoman*
5	a marketing, advertising etc. man	
6	a husband or male sexual partner	
7	US informal used when talking to someone, especially a man	
8	US slang 'the man' a person or group that has power and authority	

These definitions are related to particular roles in society in addition to relationships with and to others. Even in the definitions there appears to be a bias, both in the number of different layers of defining a man and a woman and in the ordering of these. You might have seen that the woman's role as a wife or a sexual partner appears further up the list than the corresponding male role as a husband or sexual partner. Even the examples presented to the reader subtly suggest different characteristics associated with being a man or woman. The dictionary uses the statement 'she's a really nice woman' to illustrate their definition of 'woman'. Here not only does the adjective 'nice' modify the noun 'woman' but the adverb 'really' acts as an intensifier in the noun phrase. This suggests that 'niceness' is a desirable personal quality for women. In contrast, the exemplifications for the noun 'man' focus on men's success over others, and intelligence. Look at the noun phrases 'men's champion' and 'a genius' and see how the verb phrase 'can solve' presents men as being able to give answers to problems. You might also have noted that there are far more definitions given for 'man', perhaps suggesting that there is so much more to say about men's roles and qualities.

> **KEY TERMS**
>
> **Noun phrase:** a group of words built around a noun
>
> **Verb phrase**: a group of words built around a head (main) verb

The dictionary also offers suggestions for how the word 'man' is used in informal spoken discourse. Sometimes it can be an almost generic address as in 'Hey man, how are you?' or, by choosing the definite article 'the' to precede 'man', it can express power and importance. In contrast, the ways that 'woman' can be used in speech appear to be more negative. The *Oxford English Dictionary* says that 'woman as a form of address can be used emphatically to indicate contempt, impatience', as in 'Get on with it, woman'. So linguistic equality is not just in writing but also in our informal spoken usage and this bias in language will be the focus of the next sections.

2.3 Male firstness: word order and generic terms

One of Dale Spender's key points in her book *Man Made Language* (1980) is that language is very man-centric, reflecting men's historical dominance over all areas of public and private life. Her evidence for this is the language rules created by the English grammarians from the sixteenth to the eighteenth century. These rules centred around the ideas that:

1. The male term should always come before the female one
2. Male terms should be the generic ones used to refer to all people regardless of gender and used as the 'norm'.

The first 'rule' centres on the custom in English that males tend to be mentioned first. If you address a letter to a couple in Britain, convention says that the envelope should be addressed to 'Mr' and 'Mrs' in that order. An older social practice that has mainly died out today was to use the man's name in the address, as in 'Mr and Mrs Ronald Jones'. Even now, if you search for address

2 Language and Gender

writing advice on the internet, it will offer this version as a traditional (and by implication correct) form of English social etiquette. This 'male firstness' still lives on in the Anglican marriage service. You can see this in Text 2A, an extract from the Church of England Marriage Service.

Text 2A

> Marriage is a gift of God in creation
>
> through which husband and wife may know the grace of God.
>
> It is given that as man and woman grow together in love and trust,
>
> they shall be united with one another in heart, body and mind
>
> Extract from the Church of England Marriage Service

The second 'rule' focuses on the ways that a male term can be used to represent all human beings regardless of their gender. To illustrate this, look at these two very famous examples.

- 'That's one small step for (a) man, one giant step for mankind.' (US astronaut Neil Armstrong's speech on landing on the moon in 1969)
- 'Let us therefore brace ourselves to our duties, and so bear ourselves that if the British Empire and its Commonwealth last for a thousand years, men will still say, "This was their finest hour."' (Prime Minister Winston Churchill's 1940 wartime speech to the British people)

These generic uses of 'man' are now considered very old-fashioned. In English, it's not only nouns that can be used generically. For example, in the statement 'a baby cries when he needs either food or comfort', the male pronoun 'he' here stands for all male and female babies. This type of grammatical gender is language specific, not appearing in some other European languages (such as the Uralic ones like Hungarian and Finnish) or even within the same Indo-European group of languages, since Farsi and Turkish do not use gendered pronouns.

RESEARCH QUESTION

Gendered pronouns

Using an internet search engine, research other languages that both use and do not use gendered pronouns. You could also look at languages that use/do not use gendered nouns.

Language and gender

As you do this, reflect on how grammatical gender might shape our response to the questions you were asked to consider at the start of this chapter:

- Does language influence or reflect our social reality and our views of gender?
- What assumptions could we have about languages that do not have grammatical gender?
- Does the lack of grammatical gender reflect different attitudes to gender and identity in those cultures?

2.4 Marking gender

To show how in English we can 'mark' words for gender in other ways than just by using pronouns, look at the following examples.

1   A nurse asked a patient how they were. He said, 'Are you feeling better today?'

2   The pilot taxied the plane down the runway. She called Air Traffic Control to confirm that they had permission to take off.

3   The Duke and Duchess of Cambridge raised money for charity.

4   'Are you an actress?' she was asked. 'No', she replied. 'I'm an actor.'

Think about how you responded to these. In the first two examples, did the work-related references to a 'nurse' and a 'pilot' seem to go naturally with the pronouns used? Would you have modified the occupational terms with 'male nurse' and 'female pilot'? Did you notice in examples 3 and 4 that the references to the women's title ('Duchess') and job role ('actress') contain the extra suffix *-ess*?

So by marking words either by their meaning or grammatically, we can show gendered power relations. The unmarked (or usual) term is often symbolically more powerful than the marked term. We'll be exploring these in more detail but, as an overview, we can mark terms by:

- adding suffixes to words to show that the female term has been derived from the male. English first names include examples of this. For example, *Charles/Charlotte* and *George/Georgina*

- using asymmetry, where the meanings of the address terms are not equal. For example, *master* and *mistress*

- associating job roles with a particular gender.

2 Language and Gender

> **KEY TERMS**
>
> **Unmarked term:** the regular or usual form of the term
>
> **Marked term:** the unusual form of the term, often shown by an additional suffix

2.4.1 The power of inflections

We have already started to look at how gender can be marked grammatically in English by inflectional endings such as *-ess*. These symbolise the female versions, for example in occupational roles such as *actress* and *waitress*. In this way it is clear that the unmarked form is usually male, although this is not exclusively the case. Most of these gendered suffixes originate from French and Latin, but have been affected by political correctness, where writers and speakers take steps to avoid sexist use of language.

And so through changing attitudes to sexist language, these suffixes have begun to die out. For example, 'actor' is used very consciously in the media to describe women in the acting profession in an equal manner to men. This perceived equality, however, may not be matched in the real world: there are still reported pay inequalities between male and female Hollywood actors!

But it's not just the suffix that can show inequality and present women as inferior. It can also be in the connotations of the different terms used. To show this, we can use the example of the job titles that were used for an air flight attendant. Women in this role used to be called an 'air stewardess' or 'air hostess'. Many felt that the meanings of these did not compare to those of the male counterparts, 'steward' and 'host'. You can see this from the dictionary definition given for 'steward/stewardess' in Text 2B. Note how a 'steward' is presented as in charge and is an organiser of a variety of different types of events, yet a 'stewardess' is someone who serves others in very specific situations.

Another gendered suffix *-ette* became quite popular with the British media in the 1990s. They used this suffix to denote a certain type of woman, mainly negatively. The coinages 'bachelorette' and 'ladette' were used to describe women who adopted behaviours seen by society as more masculine, like drinking, having more casual relationships with men and swearing. A British-designed TV programme *Ladette to Lady* contained the message that such women can (and should) be transformed into ladies. Here the associations with the address form 'ladies' are that this is an ideal for women and women should be 'ladies'. In this show, the contestants were taught the skills of being 'a lady'. These included being taught the right way to speak and behave, and creative skills like flower arranging and sewing.

Text 2B

steward

⭐ **a person whose job it is to organize a particular event, or to provide services to particular people, or to take care of a particular place:**

Stewards will be inspecting the race track at 9.00.

If you need help at any time during the conference, one of the stewards will be pleased to help you.

⭐ (FEMALE stewardess,) **a person who serves passengers on a ship or aircraft**

⭐ UK **a person who organizes the supply and serving of food at a club:**

He's the steward of the city of Wakefield's Working Men's Club.

Cambridge Dictionary (online) definition for 'steward'

> **KEY TERM**
> **Coinage:** the invention of a new word or phrase

Interestingly, the *-ette* suffix is used for two other purposes: as something smaller in size, as in 'kitchenette', or as imitation, for example 'leatherette'. It does not appear to be a leap to make a connection between these and the third purpose: to denote women. Obviously the most famous usage from a feminist perspective is 'suffragette'. This movement started in the late nineteenth century in Britain to obtain rights to vote for women but also reflected similar movements in America. Look at Text 2C, an extract from an American anti-suffragette leaflet titled 'Origin and Development of a Suffragette':

Text 2C

At 15 a little pet.

At 20 a little coquette.

At 40 not married yet!

At 50 a suffragette.

Extract from an anti-suffragette leaflet, 'Origin and Development of a Suffragette'

2 Language and Gender

In this, the implication is evident that for all her teasing and flirtatiousness at twenty, her lack of success with finding a husband makes her into a suffragette. This change is signalled in the nouns 'pet' and 'coquette' (a French word) modified by the adjective 'little' to describe the younger girl. Following this with the negative 'not' and the exclamative implies that she is unwanted by a man and that her last resort is to become a 'suffragette'.

2.4.2 The power of meaning

One way to signify gender lexically is through gender-specific compounding. Here two words are put together, most commonly with one being 'male/man' or 'female/woman'. Earlier we suggested that the marking of gender usually highlights where women are either inferior to their male counterpart, or where it is not the norm for women to perform this role. There are clearly some exceptions, but even these indicate that certain jobs are perhaps associated most frequently with a specific gender. Job titles like 'nurse' might be preceded by 'male', therefore identifying this role as performed mainly by women. Indeed, in her article, 'What Language Barrier?' published in *The Guardian*, Deborah Cameron explores how the 'difference model' that we looked at in Chapter 1 is still a widespread view (Cameron 2007). Cameron discusses Simon Baron-Cohen's argument in his book The Essential Difference (2003: 287) that people with a female brain 'make the most wonderful counsellors, primary school teachers, nurses, carers, therapists, social workers, mediators, group facilitators or personnel staff'. This, he says, is because they have empathy, an attribute he clearly associates with women. Using these beliefs, it therefore stands to reason that if a man does the job, the occupational role 'nurse' needs to be preceded by 'male'.

> **KEY TERM**
>
> **Compounding:** the process of word formation that joins together two or more existing words to make a new word

Other recent compounds have focused on men and these can show changing attitudes to men and masculine behaviours:

- 'Man bag' and 'man bun' mark the nouns 'bag' and 'bun' as more connected with women. Yet they also show that changing attitudes to men and fashion have affected male appearance and their accessories.

- 'Man cave' and 'he man' call upon more traditional ideas of masculinity, presenting men as still essentially hunter-gatherer cavemen.

- The 1980s phrase 'new man' suggested a type of man with a completely different attitude to traditional gender roles. 'New man' came to mean a man

Language and gender

who embraced domestic roles and participated in them whole-heartedly. The reverse of this might be seen in a compound like 'career woman' that expressly highlights the type of woman who views her job role outside of the home as an important ongoing part of her life.

- Gender-specific compounding can also be used to mock. The phrase 'man flu' is a prime example that highlights the stereotype of men exaggerating any medical ailment they have. Another recent coinage is 'mansplaining', a blend of *man + explaining*, that has come into regular usage to describe a popular, rather than academic linguistic, view of men's verbal behaviour. This is the Cambridge Dictionary's online definition: 'to explain something to someone in a way that suggests that they are stupid; used especially when a man explains something to a woman that she already understands'.

> **KEY TERM**
>
> **Blend:** a word formed from two or more parts of other already existing words

2.4.3 Addressing men and women: distinguishing titles

English titles and address terms demonstrate both the marking of gender and the lexical foregrounding of social asymmetry. The terms 'Mr', 'Mrs' and 'Miss' are signifiers of gender but for women they do even more, signalling marital status. 'Mister and 'Mr' do not denote a man's marital status unlike 'Mrs' and 'Miss' that, as titles, identify whether a woman is married or unmarried. Feminists in the 1970s did proffer an alternative 'Ms' for women to use if they wanted to avoid specifying marital status but it did not really become a popular option. Interestingly all three are abbreviations of the same historical title 'mistress'. British honorifics, as in 'Duke' and 'Duchess' or 'Viscount' and 'Viscountess' still retain the older suffixation that has disappeared from job titles like actor. Perhaps as these titles are associated with status, class and a past aristocratic feudal system, as well as used only for a small elite group of people, there is not the pressure to change them.

> **KEY TERM**
>
> **Honorifics:** a title or word expressing respect when used to address someone

In predominantly English-speaking countries, a patronymic family name system is adopted. In this a woman takes over the man's surname on marriage and

2 Language and Gender

resulting children take on this male surname as the family name. For girls, this becomes their 'maiden name', historically representing their sexual status, and the identity they lose on marriage. This is not to say that this is legally enforced and women can opt to keep their own name. In other cultures and languages, there are different approaches. Spanish naming systems seem to use a more even-handed approach as a child has a first, given name followed by two family surnames – those of both the father and mother. It used to be that it was the male surname first but gender equality laws now allow parents to choose the order. And, on marriage, women do not change their name.

One aspect of gendered language that Robin Lakoff's research highlighted was the semantic inequality and asymmetry between terms used about men and women. Lakoff cited words like *master/mistress* and *bachelor/spinster* as illustrating these. *Master* has connotations of power and control and *mistress* has a meaning of a woman with whom a man is having a sexual relationship whilst he is married. This is an example of semantic derogation, as the female term has taken on more negative connotations.

KEY TERMS

Patronymic: the element of a person's name that is based on the name of one's father, grandfather or other male ancestor

Semantic derogation: a process by which a word's meaning becomes more negative over time

2.5 Patterns and metaphors

Another way to look at how language shows our attitudes to gender is to see how we put different words together into reoccurring patterns. What happens is that these patterns seem natural to us and we overlook the gender stereotypes and bias being shown. You can practise this idea by asking yourself which of these words seem to go better with 'woman' or 'man':

- pretty
- handsome
- elegant
- powerful

You probably put 'pretty' and 'elegant' with 'woman' and 'handsome' and 'powerful' with 'man'. But ask yourself why you did this. There is no logical reason for women to be considered 'pretty' and not 'handsome'.

Language and gender

Metaphors too can help to reinforce stereotypes that already exist. Making repeated comparisons between certain objects and women and men means that we begin to associate these comparisons with something natural. We therefore believe that these comparisons are real and truthful.

> **KEY TERM**
>
> **Metaphor:** a structure that presents one thing in terms of another

2.5.1 Collocation: words that 'naturally' go together

We can also associate ideas about masculine and feminine qualities with particular words. As you read this list of words, mentally separate them into those you associate with masculine ideas and those you associate with feminine ideas:

surrender   empathy   logic   focus   nurturing   tenderness   patience

independence   control   loving   discipline   radiance   direction   strength

This list of words seems quite arbitrary and unscientific but corpus linguistics as a research tool allows linguists to quantify the patterns that they can find. And by studying corpora containing real-life language examples from a variety of text sources, researchers can identify repeated patterns. In the small-scale study of these words, you may have divided them like this (Table 2.2):

Table 2.2: Words associated with feminine and masculine ideas

Feminine	Masculine
surrender	direction
empathy	logic
nurturing	focus
tenderness	discipline
patience	independence
loving	control
radiance	strength

But through looking at patterns in a significantly greater number of texts of different types, we may find a larger discourse about gender in society. We will be exploring corpora as a methodology for gender study in Chapter 5 but Paul

2 Language and Gender

Baker's (2006) exploration of the terms 'bachelor' and 'spinster' in the British National Corpus shows how focusing on just two words can highlight the way that society views men and women.

Baker applied the concept of collocation, looking for words that seem to naturally occur with 'bachelor' and 'spinster'. In his study, one of Baker's conclusions was that 'eligible' was a common collocate of 'bachelor' and 'elderly' was a frequent collocate of 'spinster'. Perhaps unsurprisingly Baker also found positive discourse prosody, where most of the words closely associated with 'bachelor' present men in a good light. For 'spinster', he found that there was negative discourse prosody.

KEY TERMS

Collocation: a word or phrase that is usually combined together with a greater frequency than chance

Discourse prosody: the ways that seemingly neutral words can be seen as having negative or positive associations through frequent use in collocations

ACTIVITY 2.1
Categorising women

In an article from *The Daily Telegraph*, British journalist Radhika Sanghani (2017) listed 25 words that she believes are only ever applied to women. She cites examples of their use in political contexts, campaigns by celebrities such as Beyoncé and research done by *Fortune*, an American business magazine. The list contains the following words:

Airhead	Ambitious	Abrasive	Bitchy	Bolshy
Bombshell	Bossy	Breathless	Bridezilla	Bubbly
Curvy	Ditsy	Emotional	Frigid	Frumpy
High-maintenance	Hormonal	Hysterical	Illogical	Pushy
Sassy	Shrill	Voluptuous	Whinging	Working mum

You might want to look up the meanings of these words first, or you can read her article for the definitions that she gives. Once you're confident with the meanings, categorise them into different semantic fields. Here are some suggestions but you might think of others:

- emotions
- appearance
- behaviours.

Finally, reflect on the findings from your categorisations. What conclusions can you draw about views about women's characteristics and traits? What attitudes to women are being expressed?

KEY TERM
Semantic field: a group of words that fulfil the same kind of role and function in speech and writing

2.5.2 Metaphor: expressing ideologies

In their study of metaphor, George Lakoff and Mark Johnson state that 'in all aspects of life, not just in politics or love, we define our reality in terms of metaphors and then proceed to act on the basis of the metaphors' (Lakoff and Johnson 1980: 158).

This supports the ideas raised in the introduction to this chapter that language can either influence our social reality or reflect it. Undeniably, metaphors have an ideological and an evaluative effect in the judgements that we make as we use them, as we will show with some examples.

KEY TERM
Ideological: relating to a system of ideas

Linguist Janet Holmes (1994) highlights how animal metaphors for women are pervasive by demonstrating how a chicken metaphor can apply to all stages of a woman's life. She writes:

> The chicken metaphor tells the story of a girl's life. In her youth, she is a chick, and then she marries and begins feeling cooped up, so she goes

Language and Gender

to hen parties and cackles with her friends. Then she has her brood and begins to hen peck her husband. Finally, she turns into an old biddy.
(Holmes 1994: 337)

Certain animals seem to be associated with a particular gender in English. Women may be associated more with the nouns 'vixen' (a female fox), 'bitch' (a female dog) and 'bird' (which in itself is not a gendered label in English) and in adjectival form as being 'cat(ty)' or 'fox(y)'. Men might be connected more with the nouns 'rat' and 'stag'. Then, if we think about what these connote, women seem to be judged in these animal references by their behaviours towards others, as in being a 'bitch' to someone and by their appearance. For men, the connotations seem to refer to sexual behaviours. An older term for a man with sexual success would have been a 'stud' or 'stallion' referring to a male horse. Some can be applied to both men and women like 'he's a rat' and 'she looks ratty' but there is clearly some inequality in their application. The animal term, when applied to a man, links to behaviour, whereas when used for women it offers a negative comment about their physical attractiveness. Some well-known sayings, like 'are you a man or a mouse' and 'he's a pussy' make unfavourable connections to both men and women. Whilst the first example has no direct connection to women, it calls upon an understanding of a mouse's timidity and assumes that this is not a desirable masculine trait. The second example has more of a gendered focus as the noun 'pussy' is often used informally as a taboo and derogatory term for women's genitalia. The insult could be interpreted in two ways: either comparing a man to a cat, using the colloquial synonym 'pussy' and suggesting that the 'cats' are cowards and weak; or comparing a man to a woman and suggesting that this makes him less of a man. In the latter version, 'pussy' acts metonymically to represent the whole notion of a 'woman'.

KEY TERMS

Synonym: a word that has equivalent meaning to another word

Metonymy: references to things or concepts not by name but by something closely associated with them

Food is another common source for metaphors about women. As with the animal ones, you may not recognise some of the terms used as most originated from slang and informal usage and they may have now dropped out of regular usage. Here are some of the words that have been used:

crumpet   tart   sweetie   honey   sugar

You probably noticed that there seems to be a semantic field of 'sweetness' in some of the terms and the corresponding association with women and the desirability of this as a feminine trait or as a way to stereotype women. 'Crumpet' and 'tart' are both related to women in a sexual sense. 'She's a bit of crumpet' alludes to her as sexually desirable to a man and 'tart' refers to a woman deemed promiscuous and judged for her sexual behaviour. Some of these words, like 'crumpet', may be specific to British English as it refers to a savoury cake popular as a snack. Equally, in American English 'honey' and 'sugar' are used as terms of endearment, arguably used for any person regardless of gender. Comparing women to food appears to be cross-cultural and, globally, studies have found this in languages as diverse as Japanese and Tunisian Arabic.

2.6 Cleaning up language

Social shifts to more of a political correctness view of language and the recognition that there are more diverse gender identities have impacted English in a variety of ways:

- The use of non-gendered pronouns
- Making job titles gender neutral
- Particular communities taking back and reusing more positively the negative words used against them.

2.6.1 Neutralising gender: generic forms and the issues of pronouns

Synonyms like 'people' and 'everybody' have successfully replaced 'man' and 'mankind' but attempts to make pronouns gender neutral are still ongoing. There are options that you might use to avoid specifying one gender by using s/he or the plural *they*, even if this would not be grammatically correct. For people who think that the gender binary of *male/female* is too simplistic or who do not identify themselves as a man or as a woman, the third-person pronoun issues become more complex. Linguist John McWhorter (2015), in an article on the American broadcasting network CNN's website, asserts that English should adopt the new non-gendered pronoun options proposed on the Gender Neutral Pronoun Blog (www.cambridge.org/links/escgen6004). This blog suggests the following pronoun use (Table 2.3):

Table 2.3: Non-gendered pronoun options

Subject pronoun	*ze* (or *zie*)	*Ze walked home*
Object pronoun or determiner	*zir/hir*	*Ze text hir*
		Hir book

2 Language and Gender

Possessive pronoun	Zirs or Hirs	That book is zirs/hirs
Reflexive pronoun	hirself and zirself	Ze finds zirself/hirself late for work

ACTIVITY 2.2
Exploring attitudes to gender

Create a short questionnaire to find out about people's current attitudes to gender and language use.

- You could ask questions about attitudes to gendered pronouns and to specific words used about men and women.

- You can either look back to earlier in the chapter and select words that we have explored or you could think of some of your own.

If you are not a native speaker of English, you might do the equivalent for your own language to see how attitudes and patterns of associations with gender are similar or different to English. Remember to be ethical in your questionnaire design – anonymise the people involved but find out their age and gender/gender identity as this will be interesting. Collate the responses. What conclusions can you draw?

2.6.2 Gender equality and renaming

A significant social change in women's occupational roles and changing attitudes to discrimination have led to the retitling of job roles in a less gendered fashion. Institutions and professions have been particularly careful about retitling job roles so that gender is not being marked.

Here are some ways that these have been achieved:

- 'Headmaster/headmistress' has become 'principal' or 'headteacher'

- 'Fireman/firewoman' has become 'fire fighter'

- 'Policeman/policewoman' has become 'police officer'.

In these, the old practice of using suffixation to denote gender through adding 'man' or 'woman' to the job function has been replaced with more gender neutral terms. In Chapter 1, section 1.7, you were introduced to Deborah Cameron's discussion of the 'verbal hygiene' movement. The desire to clean language up is often laughed at for some of its over-the-top euphemisms – such as school dinner ladies being rebranded as education centre nourishment

Language and gender

consultants – but in taking gender out of titles there is no longer any suggestion that certain jobs are just for men.

2.6.3 Taking it back: reclaiming words

Many of the insults and taboo words used pejoratively to label minority groups are being reclaimed by the very communities they described and disparaged. This reclamation involves words being used in ways that are more culturally acceptable and positive to the affected community. In gender terms, the reclaiming of female-focused terms that appear sexist or misogynistic is having mixed success. 'Bitch' is now used (arguably) as a sisterhood term in female rap music or by a female friend to female friend. 'Butch' as a pejorative term for lesbians or heterosexual women seen as looking more masculine, has also undergone the same process and is now used within the lesbian community to describe gender identity and/or relationships. The terms 'butch' and 'femme' initially seemed to reinforce the *masculine/feminine* binary in valuing male and female characteristics but these are used by the community to show the different possible relationship configurations: 'butch-femme', 'butch-butch', etc.

Another taboo word 'slut' is having mixed success with reclamation. Calling a woman a 'slut' has always judged women by their sexual behaviour, although the word itself underwent a semantic shift. In previous meanings from earlier centuries it denoted a woman with low standards of cleanliness and a kitchen maid. Famously in 2011 a global protest movement sought to reclaim the word from its association with women's appearance as a justification for sexual violence and organised a series of 'slutwalks'. This started from a Canadian policeman's comments to university students that women should not dress like 'sluts' if they did not want to become victims of sex attacks.

KEY TERMS

Reclamation: the cultural process of removing negative associations with a particular term that has been used by a dominant group against a specific, less powerful social group

Pejorative term: a judgemental term that usually implies disapproval or criticism

Semantic shift: the changing of a word's meaning in a radically different way from its original use

Recently two English women from Essex, a county in the south-east of England, have started campaigning to remove the compound word 'Essex girl' from the

2 Language and Gender

Oxford English Dictionary (OED). Using change.org, a people-led way to air protests and views and gain popular support, the women used the slogan 'I am an Essex girl' to try and reclaim this phrase. If you want to find out more about their complaints, put their slogan into a search engine.

By looking at the *Oxford English Dictionary*'s definition, you might see why they are concerned. The OED lists the behaviours and qualities associated with being an Essex girl:

> **Essex girl n. [after Essex man n.]** Brit. derogatory a contemptuous term applied (usu. joc.) to a type of young woman, supposedly to be found in and around Essex, and variously characterized as unintelligent, promiscuous, and materialistic.

Although the OED recognises the joking nature of its usage, the women are arguing that the presence of the term in a well-respected dictionary encourages people to believe that all women from Essex are like this.

2.7 Conclusion

We started this chapter by looking at older presentations of gender in language and it is evident that much has changed. As women's roles have moved outside the home and their occupational choices have grown, language has adapted and job titles have become less gender-specific. Likewise there is more awareness of the impact of gendered language, with shifts in pronoun usage to be less male-specific showing that there is no longer a male supremacy, and also recognising the modern complexities of gender identity. Perhaps where there is still more scope for change is in terms of the words that we associate with gender and the meanings and beliefs behind these. The fact that there have been significant shifts in usage seems to suggest that changes to the social reality are now *reflected* in the language we use, although these changes were brought about in more deliberate ways as a society to shape and *influence* the ways that we think.

Wider reading

You can find out more about the topics in this chapter by reading the following:

Baker, P. (2008) *Sexed Texts: Language, Gender and Sexuality*. London: Equinox.

Mills, S. and Mullany, L. (2011) *Language, Gender and Feminism*. Abingdon: Routledge.

Sunderland, J. (2006) *Language and Gender: An Advanced Resource Book*. Abingdon: Routledge.

Chapter 3
Gender and representation

In this chapter you will:

- Understand the concept of representation

- Explore the ways that gender can be represented in different text types

- Be introduced to ways that gendered social actors can be represented

- Investigate the notion of gendered discourses

3 Language and Gender

3.1 Introduction

In this chapter, the focus is specifically on representation, the ways in which text producers use meaning-making resources like language, images and objects to portray (or represent) people, events or situations. Representation is connected with society's ways of seeing the world and can be seen in all kinds of texts around us. Most obviously, issues of gendered representations of women and men surround us in the media and in advertisements. But it's not just in the media or commercial spheres. Representation can also be relevant to other modes and contexts. Take spoken language where, for example, politicians in their speeches might allude to issues connected with gender. Or in computer-mediated contexts like social media sites, gender might be represented in a certain way depending on the writer's beliefs or the intended audience. So exploring representation continues the earlier debate about whether gendered meanings are *created* in response to social attitudes and beliefs or frame and *shape* these attitudes and beliefs.

And, on a wider level, repeated representations can create discourses, a term defined by Michel Foucault (1972: 49) as 'practices which systematically form the objects of which they speak'.

> **KEY TERMS**
>
> **Representation:** the portrayal of events, people and circumstances through language and other meaning-making resources (e.g. images and sound) to create a way of seeing the world
>
> **Discourses:** combining meaning-making resources to present particular ways of seeing the world

What Foucault is drawing to our attention is that repeated practices, often language use, create another layer of meaning. Discourses, too, offer ways of seeing the world and are clearly relevant to the study of language and gender. The language that writers and speakers use can encode specific attitudes to gender and position readers or listeners to accept or reject the discourse with which they are presented.

3.2 Exploring gender and discourse

According to Jane Sunderland (2004), discourses can be given specific names, for example an *equal opportunities* or *political correctness* discourse could

Gender and representation

exist in relation to gender. Therefore, an organisation might issue guidelines to its staff about acceptable pronouns (*he, she, they*) to use in communications with customers or about appropriate address terms (*Mr, Miss, Ms*) that can be used or not in order not to exclude people on the basis of gender or marital status. Additionally, Sunderland suggests that discourses can have certain functions. Some of the functions that she identifies are:

- **Resistant**: a discourse that challenges accepted views
- **Subversive**: a discourse that undermines accepted views
- **Conservative**: a discourse that shows a more traditional and unchallenging attitude
- **Progressive**: a forward-thinking discourse

She also highlights the ways that discourses can exist alongside other ones, becoming *competing, dominant, co-existing* or *alternative*, etc. In a particular society, a *dominant* discourse might be a *conservative* one that it is still more appropriate for women to stay at home and care for their children. If there is another discourse that working mothers can be a positive influence for children, then this could be a *competing, co-existing* or *alternative* discourse – depending on where, how and by whom these discourses were presented.

What this means is that there may not be one single discourse about gender at any one time but a range of discourses that depend upon these questions:

- Who has produced the text?
- What are their motivations?
- Who is the implied or intended audience?
- What type of text is being produced?
- What is the intended purpose?

3.3 Semiotics: signs and gender

One of the key ways that we see gender enacted in the world is through the signs that surround us. Just as we started by exploring the semantic distinctions between biological sex and gender, there is the equivalent difference in the symbols that can be used to represent male and female. In biological terms, the combined graphemes XX and XY represent women and men with their origin lying in scientific classification.

Ferdinand de Saussure's early twentieth-century concept of semiology explores the link between a signifier (the thing that carries or produces meaning) and the

Language and Gender

signified (the meaning itself or the mental concept). Saussure took a linguistic focus and considered this in respect to words. So the nouns 'man' and 'woman' act as the signifiers and the signified are our mental concepts of what a man and a woman are. For example, the dictionary definitions in Chapter 2 suggest some of the meanings we give to those particular nouns.

A later theorist, Roland Barthes, expanded upon Saussure's views to incorporate images. For both Saussure and Barthes, meanings are not a natural result of what we see but are often (although not exclusively) culturally specific. Barthes divided his signs into their denotations and their connotations, i.e. the cultural meanings that we give to them.

> **KEY TERMS**
>
> **Grapheme:** the smallest unit of the writing system such as the letter of the alphabet
>
> **Semiology:** the study of signs
>
> **Signifier:** the form which the sign takes, for example, a word or an image
>
> **Signified:** the mental concept associated with the sign
>
> **Denotation:** what a word stands for in its most literal sense
>
> **Connotation:** the aura of emotional meaning that we associate with a word

For example, look at Figure 3.1, which shows the symbols commonly used to represent the genders of man and woman. On the left is the symbol for man and on the right is the corresponding symbol for woman.

Figure 3.1: Symbols for male and female

Gender and representation

The 'denoted' images are simply man and woman and the connotations are all our notions of masculinity and femininity. The male gender is represented through the Mars planetary symbol and the female gender through the Venus one. We have already seen how the terms 'Mars' and 'Venus' were used in a popular book to explain men and women's differences, but now you can see how these were already linked to men and women symbolically in a visual way. Add into the mix the colours – blue for men and pink for women – and we have the modern and highly recognisable English cultural binary representations of gender encoded in symbols of images, colour and their connotations.

3.3.1 Toilet signs and gender

One aspect of our social experience where gender separation is most evident in the world around us is in public toilets. Toilet signs thus provide interesting examples of the link between the signifiers and the signified. Pictograms for men and women are based on depictions of body shapes, dress styles and body parts. Look at Figure 3.2 to see this in practice.

In these signs, a way to represent gender is through clothing, with men in suits and women in dresses. Physical shapes often emphasise differences between the genders, emphasising the stereotypes of muscly men and slim women. Also, non-verbal features such as gesture, facial expression and body posture all represent perceptions of masculinity and femininity. In other signs, attempts at humour variously show men looking over the toilet door at the women's cubicles or use jokes – as in one sign which reads 'men to the left because women are always right'.

Figure 3.2: Different toilet signs

3 Language and Gender

Toilet signs can sometimes just use an image or a word, or else combine the two to create the meaning. Whatever the visual representation, meaning-making occurs by using our cultural knowledge to interpret the signified. Toilets too are a site of changing gender attitudes as gender neutral ones now feature in educational establishments and workplaces. The sign in Figure 3.3 directly addresses this equality issue by saying 'All gender restroom'.

Figure 3.3: Gender neutral toilet sign

ACTIVITY 3.1
Exploring gendered toilet signs

Look at Table 3.1 which offers a selection of the toilet signs found using an online search. You could make this activity more visual by conducting your own image search for toilet signs. Consider these questions:

- What metaphors or cultural references are being used?

- Do the representations seem equal? If not, where is the imbalance and what creates this?

Table 3.1: Examples of text used for different toilet signs

Women	Men
Mermaids	Neptune
	Pirates
	Sailors
Wonder Woman	Batman
Ladies	Fellas
Red Riding Hood	Big Bad Wolf
Dollfaces	Old Sports (from F. Scott Fitzgerald's novel *The Great Gatsby*)

3.4 Representing gender through metaphor

Activity 3.1 explored how metaphors can illustrate representations of maleness and femaleness. You could see this with the metaphorical allusions to fairy tale and film characters used within the toilet signs. Using an approach from cognitive linguistics, we can think of metaphors as conceptual metaphors and consider the ways that we can map how writers and speakers express the concept of gender and what seems to be the essence of being female or male. In order to map these (and find patterns), we can divide our metaphors into two areas:

- target domain: the concept that is understood through another domain of knowledge (source domain)
- source domain: a domain of knowledge used as a vehicle for understanding another concept (target domain).

KEY TERMS

Cognitive linguistics: the study of language that draws on insights from cognitive science

Conceptual metaphor: a structure that presents one concept in terms of another

3 Language and Gender

> **Target domain:** the abstract concept/area of knowledge that is understood in terms of a more concrete one
>
> **Source domain:** a concrete area of knowledge that is used to understand an abstract concept

To show how this can be applied, let's look at a nineteenth-century English nursery rhyme that offers metaphorical representations for both genders. Text 3A shows an abbreviated version.

Text 3A

> What are little boys made of?/frogs and snails and puppy dog tails
>
> What are little girls made of?/sugar and spice and all things nice
>
> What are young men made of?/sighs and leers and crocodile tears
>
> What are young women made of?/ribbons and lace and sweet pretty faces

The source domain for girls is food ('sugar and spice'), an association already noted as typical. For young women, this changes to small decorative items of clothing ('ribbons and lace') and the shifting of the source domain to one of external appearance is shown in the noun phrase 'sweet pretty faces'. Even here the modifier 'sweet' still retains a food association. For boys, there is an assumption that the source domain is animals, and presumably ones chosen for their unpleasantness ('frogs and snails'); in a similar vein, other versions of the rhyme use slugs and snakes as variations for the animals. The verse for young men suggests a source domain based around sexual behaviour with the 'sighs and leers' and falseness in the animal metaphor of 'crocodile tears'. We can see that by looking at the textual function of specific metaphors we can identify clusters and patterns which offer evidence of stereotypes and constructed social roles for gendered participants, even at an early age. In this rhyme social roles for young men are built around sexual behaviours and for young women around the way that they look.

3.5 Gender and power

One of our big debates so far has been the extent to which gender is a social practice rather than something innate. This leads nicely into a focus on gender from the point of view of one theoretical approach, that of Critical Discourse Analysis (CDA). A CDA approach, grounded in its focus on the nature of social

Gender and representation

power, attempts to make links between gender and ideological aspects of power, dominance and inequality in society. Earlier we considered 'dominance' as explaining male and female spoken interactions and now we can explore if ideas of male dominance are represented in literary texts. Using CDA, differences between representations of men and women can be explored, along with the 'discourses' that these then promote.

> **KEY TERM**
>
> **Critical Discourse Analysis (CDA):** an approach to studying language that focuses on aspects of social power and inequality in text and talk

3.5.1 Exploring the representation of masculinity and femininity in literature

A literary genre famous for representing men and women in gender stereotypical ways is that of the romance novel. It's a genre that does not seem to have updated representations in line with social change. Romance novels are very formulaic with the same broad representations of masculinity and femininity repeated in similar scenarios by different writers. These are understood by readers who are aware of these stereotypical representations and expect them to be maintained. The roles given to characters within this genre reflect a dominance/power model since, in many cases, hierarchical positions are used as a plot device to represent men as more powerful than women. One repeated scenario is romance within a workplace context, where the man is positioned as the CEO of an organisation and the woman is often his secretary.

> **ACTIVITY 3.2**
>
> **Investigating representations of masculinity and dominance**
>
> Text 3B is an extract from Thomas Hardy's *Tess of the D'Urbervilles*. It features an encounter between Alec D'Urberville and Tess Durbeyfield. The novel was written in the nineteenth century and is set in a rural part of England. Tess is a young girl who comes from a poor family and works on farms as a milkmaid. Her parents encourage her to meet the D'Urbervilles, a rich local family because they think that they might be related (something that is not true). Alec, the son, is attracted to Tess and attempts to seduce her. Here he is driving her in his carriage.

3 Language and Gender

Read Text 3B and then answer these questions:

- Analyse the presentation of masculinity and femininity in this extract. How are the different statuses of the characters presented?
- Explore the descriptions of Alec's behaviour towards Tess and his assertions of dominance. How does the language he uses in direct speech represent his masculinity?

Text 3B

He loosened rein, and away they went a second time. D'Urberville turned his face to her as they rocked, and said, in playful raillery: "Now then, put your arms round my waist again, as you did before, my Beauty."

"Never!" said Tess independently, holding on as well as she could without touching him.

"Let me put one little kiss on those holmberry lips, Tess, or even on that warmed cheek, and I'll stop—on my honour, I will!"

Tess, surprised beyond measure, slid farther back still on her seat, at which he urged the horse anew, and rocked her the more.

"Will nothing else do?" she cried at length, in desperation, her large eyes staring at him like those of a wild animal. This dressing her up so prettily by her mother had apparently been to lamentable purpose.

"Nothing, dear Tess," he replied.

"Oh, I don't know—very well; I don't mind!" she panted miserably.

He drew rein, and as they slowed he was on the point of imprinting the desired salute, when, as if hardly yet aware of her own modesty, she dodged aside. His arms being occupied with the reins there was left him no power to prevent her manoeuvre.

"Now, damn it—I'll break both our necks!" swore her capriciously passionate companion. "So you can go from your word like that, you young witch, can you?"

"Very well," said Tess, "I'll not more since you be so determined! But I—thought you would be kind to me, and protect me, as my kinsman!"

"Kinsman be hanged! Now!"

"But I don't want anybody to kiss me, sir!" she implored, a big tear beginning to roll down her face, and the corners of her mouth trembling in her attempts not to cry. "And I wouldn't ha' come if I had known!"

Gender and representation

He was inexorable, and she sat still, and d'Urberville gave her the kiss of mastery. No sooner had he done so than she flushed with shame, took out her handkerchief, and wiped the spot on her cheek that had been touched by his lips. His ardour was nettled at the sight, for the act on her part had been unconsciously done.

Extract from *Tess of the D'Urbervilles*, Thomas Hardy (1891: Chapter 8)

3.6 Gender and social actor representation

As a theoretical model, Theo Van Leeuwen's Social Actor Network (1996) offers us a useful framework to investigate both representations and discourses. In this model, he places emphasis on the participants presented either in the text or the interaction, calling them the social actors. Theo Van Leeuwen's network model offers a detailed sub-categorisation of social actors, allowing for a more detailed analysis of:

- *what* groups and individuals are referred to
- *how* they are referred to.

In his categories, he connects their functions with the language used to construct these. He has many of these categories but we will only explore some of the most helpful ones in identifying the representation of women and men. One of Van Leeuwen's main aspects of representation is through nomination (the naming of the social actor) but within this he labels further categories:

- **Functionalisation**: the roles and occupations held by the social actor
- **Classification**: aspects of identity, such as class, age and gender
- **Relational identification**: relationship to others, such as family or work connections
- **Physical identifications**: aspects of appearance.

KEY TERMS

Social Actor Network: an analytical framework of categorising how social actors are represented

Nomination: the process of naming

3 Language and Gender

Imagine a newspaper headline that read '20-year-old blonde primary teacher Gemma married famous author Anthony Howat in secret ceremony'. If you break this down, you can see how this highlights how Van Leeuwen's categories can be applied.

We have just seen that social actors can be represented through *nomination*, where the social actor's name or identity is used, but this can take different forms:

- **Formalisation**: shown through surname only or with titles/honorifics
- **Semi-formalisation**: shown through using both surname and first name
- **Informalisation:** where the first name only is used.

Another method of representation is collectivisation, where social actors are referred to as a group with plural grammatical forms. We will explore these forms and the various categories in media texts.

3.6.1 Gender and social actor representation in the media

So, to explore representation and discourses further, we could return to the idea raised in the introduction of women's family and work roles still being a topic of interest and debate. This is certainly an area that the British media report on regularly, presumably in the belief that their audiences are interested too. As you read these headlines from the same source, reflect on how these represent women as social actors.

1. The poisonous legacy of Superwoman lives on today: feminist career women demand jobs for ALL women, but could that view damage the lives of mothers and their children?
2. Why career women should definitely LIE about having a family: mother-of-three says admitting to your boss that you have kids is a dangerous business.
3. Working mothers risk damaging their child's future prospects.
4. Children of working mothers fall behind those of stay-at-home mums.
5. Working mothers have FATTER children: recent rise in obesity rates among children is blamed on women going out to work.

Even without applying any linguistic analysis, it's likely that you have identified the negativity in the representation. Perhaps this stems from the terms 'career women' and 'working mothers' as marked ones. If you think of the possible male equivalents, 'career men' and 'working fathers', these do not seem to work as natural collocates.

In the headlines you may now have noted that the women are not *nominated* but are *functionalised* in roles and collectivised, for example in plural terms as

Gender and representation

'career women' and 'working mothers' or as 'stay-at-home mums'. There is, however, what van Leeuwen calls 'relational identification'. This is where social actors are represented in terms of their personal or work relationships with each other and it is realised linguistically by a closed set of nouns denoting these relations – 'husband', 'uncle', 'colleague' would be examples for men. In the headlines, the key relational identification is in reference to the mothers' children, using the possessive form 'their child/children' to activate the relationship.

When looking at social actors, van Leeuwen also makes much of the *inclusion* (who takes part) and *exclusion* (who's left out). Interestingly, the social actors excluded from these headlines are the fathers. By not mentioning them they have been suppressed; it is as if they have no responsibility for their children. But this also has the effect of placing blame for children's obesity or lack of success on the working mother. Apparent throughout is the functionalisation.

Gender is foregrounded in these headlines. The semantic choices also highlight the negative effects of women's life choices in the associations of harm in the verbs 'damage', 'risk damaging' and the adjectives 'dangerous' and 'poisonous'. The headlines also have a declarative function making these appear as facts, despite the fact that the assertion that working women have fatter children is not supported.

3.6.2 Introducing social actor representation and verb processes

One important element of Theo Van Leeuwen's model is whether social actors are either *activated* or *passivated*.

- Activation occurs when the social actor is represented as the active, forceful element in an activity.

- Passivation happens when the social actor is represented as undergoing an activity or as being the receiver of an action or event. (This is not to be confused with the passive voice.)

In this model, the nature of agency is important; we can use Michael Halliday's categories of verb processes to help our analyses of social actor representation. This is because these focus on how particular meanings can be created and relationships between participants can be shown through the verbs used. But it is also useful for looking at power and dominance, so could be applied when taking a CDA approach too.

The verb processes can be categorised in the following ways:

- Material verb process: a process which is about what is going on outside the participant. Verbs used here are associated with actions and doing and involve one participant (called the agent) doing something to another participant (usually called the object).

3 Language and Gender

- **Mental verb process**: a process which is about inner experience. Verbs used here are ones associated with the human senses of thinking, perception (like seeing and hearing) and feelings.

- **Verbal verb process**: a process which is about the exchange of meaning through 'saying'. Verbs used here are associated with communication.

- **Relational verb process**: a process which is about classifying and identifying experiences through the use of verbs like being, becoming or having.

KEY TERMS

Activation: where the social actor is the active forceful element in an activity

Passivation: where the social actor is the receiver of an action or event

Agency: the one who is doing, often identified by the grammatical agent as the subject

Material verb process: verbs associated with actions and doing

Mental verb process: verbs associated with thinking and feeling, or with perception

Verbal verb process: verbs associated with saying and communicating

Relational verb process: verbs associated with being, becoming or having

ACTIVITY 3.3

Exploring gender and social actor representation in literature

Text 3C is an excerpt from 'The Yellow Wallpaper', a short story written in 1892 by Charlotte Perkins Gilman. The narrative depicts an unnamed female narrator's struggles with her mental health after the birth of her child. It also presents a response to being confined by her family in an attic room with barred windows in the belief that this will help her recovery. Read the text, and consider the following questions.

- Who are the social actors and how are they nominated? How are they functionalised, classified and identified relationally?

- Who is activated and passivated? In what ways?

Gender and representation

- What types of verb processes do you see used in relation to the different social actors?
- From your analysis, how are the characters represented in a gendered way?

Text 3C

John laughs at me, of course, but one expects that in marriage.

John is practical in the extreme. He has no patience with faith, an intense horror of superstition, and he scoffs openly at any talk of things not to be felt and seen and put down in figures.

John is a physician, and PERHAPS—(I would not say it to a living soul, of course, but this is dead paper and a great relief to my mind)—PERHAPS that is one reason I do not get well faster.

You see he does not believe I am sick!

And what can one do?

If a physician of high standing, and one's own husband, assures friends and relatives that there is really nothing the matter with one but temporary nervous depression—a slight hysterical tendency—what is one to do?

My brother is also a physician, and also of high standing, and he says the same thing.

So I take phosphates or phosphites—whichever it is, and tonics, and journeys, and air, and exercise, and am absolutely forbidden to 'work' until I am well again.

Personally, I disagree with their ideas.

Personally, I believe that congenial work, with excitement and change, would do me good.

But what is one to do?

Extract from 'The Yellow Wallpaper', Charlotte Perkins Gilman (1892)

3.7 Different discourses about gender

By comparing the *discourses* about men and women who choose to go against a perceived social norm by staying at home or going to work, we can see if these have a *conservative* function, according to Sunderland's definitions outlined at

Language and Gender

the start of this chapter. It is likely that the nature of the newspaper source will determine whether there is a more conservative and traditional point of view of social roles represented. Arguably issues of parenting and childcare are made into a gendered discourse rather than being a discourse on gender. This means that in practice, a non-gender issue (who works and who doesn't) is being gendered and positioning women and men in certain ways. However, to see whether there are competing discourses about fatherhood/masculinity and career choices and the equivalent for mothers, we would need to explore a range of texts. For example, parenting magazines, internet forums and newspapers could be sources of data for you to explore in more detail and confirm or contest ideas we have discussed here.

ACTIVITY 3.4
Investigating gendered discourses

To investigate discourses further, look at these headlines representing 'stay-at-home' fathers. Then answer the questions.

1. Why don't more dads choose to stay at home? The answer is that they get bullied and are made to feel inadequate by yummy mummies.

2. Stay-at-home fathers double in 20 years: now over 200,000 look after their children. As Britain's economy shrinks, is it the recession or a man-cession that keeps them there?

3. You can never fancy a man who becomes a house husband or stay-at-home dad: In Carina's world he was the family breadwinner and she raised the children. When Carina and her husband swapped roles, he lost his sex appeal and his wife.

4. The stay-at-home dad who says he lost not only his dignity but his children's respect: Once Jackson Jones used to be in charge of an annual budget of a million pounds, now he struggles to balance his monthly household bills and his family are not happy.

5. Richard Leigh was so proud to be a stay-at-home dad. Now he fears it's harmed both his son and his daughter.

- How are the social actors identified? How is this achieved through lexical and grammatical choices?

- Overall, what kind of discourse is there about men who stay at home to look after their children?

Gender and representation

3.8 Gender representation in the media: health magazines

Now let's look at the media texts in Texts 3D and 3E, to see how representations and discourses change for women and men, even when the topic is the same. Health is an issue that should be of concern to all, but two separate websites exist to advertise the same publisher's magazines aimed at each gender. Arguably, given that some biological differences do exist, this may not be surprising but investigating how and if these differences are presented will be interesting.

Text 3D

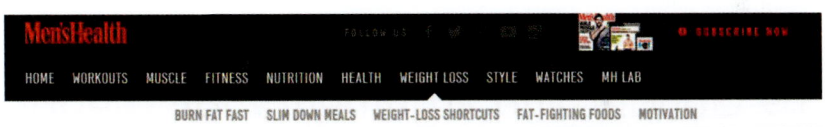

Banner for *Men's Health* magazine website

Text 3E

Banner for *Women's Health* magazine website

Most noticeably from a visual perspective, the colours black and red dominate the banner used for *Men's Health*, which contrasts with the white and orange for *Women's Health*. Indeed, the choice of white text on black is reversed for women. Typographically, the fonts are dissimilar and the placement of the titles foregrounds that it's about the issue of health for women (as it's centred on the page) but downplays it for men (it's more hidden away at the top left of the page). The links to social media for *Men's Health* represent men as more technological, unlike women who have the more traditional option of a newsletter.

As the direction of English reading and writing is left to right we can see immediately that there is a hierarchy of importance and interest suggested by what the readers will read first. This convention creates the discourse structure, placing greater emphasis on fitness in *Men's Health* with three different headings of 'workouts', 'muscle' and 'fitness' that connote masculine attitudes to fitness. For women,

53

3 Language and Gender

'beauty and fashion' appear before the 'style' equivalent for men, representing a stereotypical femininity of concern for appearance – even before health.

Within the sub-category of weight loss there appear more differences, with men being represented as valuing speed ('fast', 'shortcuts') and as being driven by eliminating fat in the desire for 'muscle'. So the alliterative 'burn fat fast' and 'fat-fighting foods' suggest this as a key goal for men. For women, 'burn' is not used as an imperative verb, but shifts to become a noun ('fat burners'), making the activity appear less active and engaged. The goal for women is expressed in the imperative 'stay slim forever' where the adjective is a complement of the verb, whereas for men the adjective 'slim' appears as a modifier for 'meals'. 'Weight loss stories' represents women as needing the support of other people's experiences and enjoyed sharing whereas for men, the option of 'motivation' implies that they may be more interested in the abstract qualities of this and do not require support from other people.

3.9 Gender and argumentation theory

You could use argumentation theory, a framework which considers the arguments used to justify particular courses of action. This stems from the Ancient Greek tradition of logical reasoning. This is relevant to our focus on discourses and representation. We can see how either the argument presented or the actions suggested may reflect or respond to the discourses around certain gendered groups. Within argumentation, the key elements are:

- **Premises:** or a set of assumptions
- **Implications**: what the possible effects are based on the assumptions
- **Presupposition**: assumptions that are based on assumed shared background knowledge that are not necessarily proved.

> **KEY TERM**
>
> **Argumentation theory:** the study of how conclusions can be reached through logical reasoning

3.9.1 Applying argumentation to gender and educational discourses

A recent educational gendered discourse surrounds the general underachievement of boys in English schools compared to that of girls. This is reported on by Ofsted, the organisation that inspects and passes judgement on the success of all English schools. Here the *premise* of the recommendations

Gender and representation

made in an Ofsted summary report from 2003 (updating a previous one called *The Gender Divide* from 1996) suggests that if the required actions by teachers and schools are taken to address boys' specific learning needs, then their examination results and overall achievement will improve. The *implication* is that unless boys' underachievement is addressed then they will continue to fail. These statements all contain *presuppositions*, based on how boys are perceived and represented as a group. As you read Ofsted's recommendations in Text 3F, reflect on what you think their presuppositions are.

Text 3F

> Making sure the school has a strong ethos where pupils and staff show respect for each other and offer plenty of extra-curricular activities, thereby making the school a place where boys feel they belong.
>
> Implementing behaviour and discipline policies firmly but equitably, with good pastoral support, so the school is a place where boys feel comfortable with learning.
>
> Using staff development to raise awareness of pupils' different learning styles and helping boys to organise their independent work by giving more frequent, shorter deadlines.
>
> Improving the quality of teaching and classroom management, thus helping teachers to gain the respect and attention of boys.
>
> Monitoring pupils' progress against benchmarks and targets, and intervening early so boys' problems are addressed before they cause demotivation.
>
> Increasing the range and extent of learning support available for pupils and tackling low self-esteem among boys by helping them with organisation.

What you might have concluded from this are that the presuppositions seem concerned with boys' educational needs as different from girls'. The statements suggest that boys:

- learn in different ways and they need extra support to help them achieve
- are active and need extra-curricular activities outside the classroom to make them feel part of a school community
- need teachers to deliver high-quality lessons in order to get them to learn and for teachers to treat all students in the same way for boys to accept disciplinary decisions
- will only give respect if it is earned
- cannot organise themselves and require extra support than teachers to help them achieve.

3 Language and Gender

We have not looked at how these are realised in the language used but you could reflect on how the presuppositions are encoded in the nouns like 'demotivation', 'respect', 'attention' and 'organisation' and the emphasis on how boys 'feel'. Boys are as a group, throughout this report, presented as being different to girls, with their own needs and special, as worthy of a whole section. However, this is within a context of their lack of success compared to that of girls and so discourses are always of their own time; this is a current issue and may not be the same in the future.

> **RESEARCH QUESTION**
> Your own research
>
> There is much scope for pursuing your own investigations into some of the areas we have discussed so far. You could explore:
>
> - Representation of women in the workplace
>
> - Gendered discourses in the media (newspapers, magazines, advertising) and on internet parenting forums
>
> - Changing representations of women in young adult fiction such as *The Hunger Games*.
>
> You could also find academic papers, short chapters in collections or whole books written by linguists in these areas that would develop your understanding. See the wider reading list at the end for some suggestions or use sites such as Google Scholar or academia.edu.
>
> To give you a focus for analysis, review this chapter for the theories and concepts we have covered and look closely at the sections of detailed analysis of individual texts. Think about what would be interesting in lexical/semantic or grammatical choices to probe further in your own research.

3.10 Gender representation in corpus data: talking and writing about sportspeople

From a linguistic perspective, a very effective way to explore gender representation is to use a corpus approach. What's possible in this approach is to process information from lots of different text types quickly and efficiently and to draw conclusions based on real data.

Gender and representation

In 2016, the year of the Brazil Olympics, Cambridge University Press published a report titled *Language, Gender and Sport*. This was compiled from three different corpora:

1. The Cambridge English Corpus (CEC), a multi-billion word collection of English language from a variety of contexts and genres, and covering both the spoken and written modes
2. The Sports Corpus, a 150 million-word subset of the CEC created by the tagging of the subject 'sport'
3. The Olympics Corpus, created as the Rio Olympics took place and using seed words and specific URLs.

> **KEY TERM**
>
> **Seed words:** a list of words directly related to the topic that are used in the corpus search

Figure 3.4 illustrates how the Cambridge English Corpus and Olympics corpus compared in their usage of three terms: sportsman, sportswoman and sportsperson.

Figure 3.4: Comparing corpora

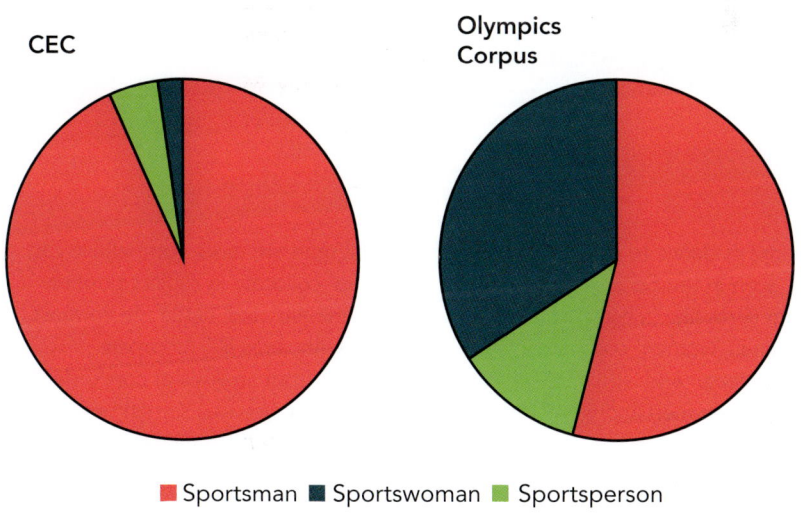

3 Language and Gender

There were a number of key findings:

- Despite 'sportsman' appearing more frequently, the frequencies of 'sportsman/sportswoman/sportsperson' were considerably more balanced in the Olympics Corpus.

- Particularly significant was the relatively high usage of the gender neutral term 'sportsperson'. The report explains this as a deliberate attempt to address the sexist reporting that had previously been a feature of sports journalism and commentary.

- The significantly more mentions of female athletes in the Olympics Corpus than the Cambridge Corpus may reflect the increasing participation of women in Olympic sports, as well as the tendency to mark women's sport more than men's.

The report also found that there was a focus on women's appearance and men's behaviours in relation to sport in the Sports Corpus. Here, 'women' collocated with 'clad', as in 'scantily clad', and also with the verb 'dress'. Further evidence of this was found in the Olympics Corpus, where a word sketch for 'women' shows a strong collocation with the verb 'wear'. Other findings were that, in the Sports Corpus, 'married' and 'unmarried' are top collocations for 'women', but not 'men'. Age too was a factor for women, but not for men.

> **KEY TERMS**
>
> **Gender neutral terms:** words or phrases that avoid bias towards a particular gender
>
> **Word sketch:** a short corpus-created summary of a word's collocational behaviour that has been automatically generated

Some evidence to support the perception that men are more competitive can be seen in the Sports Corpus. Here 'men/man' collocate in subject position with verbs like 'mastermind', 'beat', 'win', 'dominate' and 'battle'. In contrast, 'woman/women' collocate in subject position with verbs like 'compete', 'participate' and 'strive'. As the report highlights from analysis of concordances, even when men and women win, a different verb choice was sometimes used, for example, women 'clinch' titles, men 'claim' theirs; this seems to present women as having more of a struggle to achieve a title than men.

Gender and representation

> **PRACTICE QUESTION**
>
> Comparing discourse
>
> To compare representations and discourses, use the headlines about women in section 3.6.1 and the headlines about men in Activity 3.4.
>
> - What similarities or differences are there between the discourses about women who work and men who stay at home?
> - Are the discourses competing or alternative ones? Do they challenge a conservative or accepted discourse?
> - Use specific examples of language to support your points.

3.11 Conclusion

If you look at old print-based or television advertisements for products you can see that representations of gender have changed over time, reflecting changing social attitudes. This highlights the way that representations aren't fixed but can alter. And, in our modern digital world and global culture, it's easy to find varied and competing discourses about gender. One aspect that you might feel that we haven't considered in a time of social media and the selfie is that of self-representation. Given that we have already considered gender from a social-constructionist perspective as a 'performance', then exploring the different meaning-making symbols that individuals use to represent themselves in both a gendered and non-gendered manner would be interesting. In the next chapter, we will be drawing attention to gender and identity, and how the technology at our personal disposal allows us to consider how we want to present ourselves as individuals to the world.

Wider reading

You can find out more about the concepts and ideas in this chapter by reading these books:

Fine, C. (2010) *Delusions of Gender: The Real Science Behind Sex Differences*. London: Icon.

Koller, V. (2008) 'CEOs and "working gals": the textual representation and cognitive conceptualisation of businesswomen in different discourse communities'. In K. Harrington, L. Litosseliti, H. Sauntson, and J. Sunderland, (eds) *Gender and Language Research Methodologies*. Basingstoke: Palgrave Macmillan.

Sunderland, J. (2004) *Gendered Discourses*. Basingstoke: Palgrave Macmillan.

Chapter 4
Gender and identity

In this chapter you will:

- Explore ideas about gender and identity

Gender and identity

4.1 Introduction

Much of the way that we can both think about ourselves and describe ourselves is through binary oppositions. Are we old or young, black or white, rich or poor? Do we live in the east or west, north or south? In gender terms, are we a man or a woman? Our answers to these all combine to give us our sense of personal identity. Perhaps using the plural 'identities' is more accurate, because there is no one single identity that completely defines us. Likewise we can shift between identities as we move through our daily lives. Think about how you change your identity as you interact with different people, in different situations and for different purposes.

This suggests that our identity is not 'fixed'; the experiences that we gather through our lives can change our identity. Becoming a parent, having a specific job role and aging can all alter our sense of who we are. However, one key factor that influences our identity is our gender. We may see this identity in a fixed sense or as a shifting one in our modern world, which is more aware of complex gender and sexuality issues and where binary distinctions are less evident.

KEY TERM

binary oppositions: a pair of related terms that are opposite in meaning

ACTIVITY 4.1
Exploring identities

A good place to start with thinking about identity is to look at yourself and reflect on the kind of identities you present to your family, friends and the other people that you are networked with.

Survey your online accounts: Twitter, Facebook, Instagram, Snapchat and any blogs or forums you contribute to. Look at the following questions and ask yourself how each of these creates or presents aspects of you.

- What do your Facebook 'likes' or the people or organisations on Twitter that you follow say about you?
- What kinds of things do you post about or comment upon?
- What about the visual images you post?

4 Language and Gender

4.2 Identity in discourse: socially constructed selves in private talk

One of the current approaches to the study of gender and language is social constructivism. What's important in this approach is the ways that the language we use constructs (or creates) gender. This contrasts to the previous theoretical approaches that concentrated on language as reflecting gender and the differences between men and women's language choices, and suggested that we speak in a certain way because we are female or male. Central to social constructivism is the focus on what is communicated *by*, *to* and *about* women and men.

4.2.1 Exploring identity and the social constructed self

Look at Text 4A, an interaction between a mother and her son Charlie, aged 16. This took place at home at the dining table, a place commonly used to interact as a family. It was not a spontaneous interaction but was set up by the mother who wanted to record her son for a project on regional accents. Her task was to get her son to talk for about ten minutes. Although the talk is not about gender, it raises some issues of identity and gender in the content of the talk. In this talk, they discuss Charlie's enjoyment of football, both playing it for a local team and casually with friends as a leisure activity.

As you read, reflect on the ways the talk, its content and the style link to ideas of gender as being constructed:

1   in an active way (by the speakers)

2   interactively (through communicating with others)

3   in a negotiated manner (as speakers come to an understanding between them).

Text 4A

Mum: you can talk about football

Charlie: yeah cos I've spent about six hours just watching it today when I should have been revising I spent six hours watching it I couldn't couldn't get away from it (.) I've got to watch it to see if Leicester win the league (.) I'm literally just such a generic little teenager aren't I [*Mum laughs*] just your typical teenager I enjoy it (.) it's good isn't it like (.) seeing everyone especially playin' for Signal cos I see all my Maple lads then

Gender and identity

Mum: well you like playing it more than watching it (.) because you haven't really got a team you've given up Chelsea now

Charlie: yeah [*laughs*] I'm not gonna lie I just I don't I don't see the point in supporting them anymore I'd rather just (.) you know watch it and just enjoy (.) it all (.) but it is more what I'm in to because sometimes (.) sometimes I get such an urge to play football it's really weird so I can't wait to have my car and drive to Wardley and go and play football it'll be so good (2.) but it's a bit (.) of effort like getting up this morning was the worst thing (.) it's effort now cos it's different going from playing (.) under 11 and stuff (.) and now going to under 16s no one cares like today (.) you know how we won it was like our first win of the season and it was against nine men that's why we won (.) because we were playin' a team with nine men [*laughs*] it's the only reason we won [*Mum laughs*] an' when I tell Oscar about it I exclude that information

Mum: you do

Charlie: when I'm going to school I texted Oscar before sayin' we won 4–2 (.) but I'm not going to mention that they only had nine players and we had eleven [*Mum laughs*] but it's a bit sad to be honest but then it's also nice at the same time it's (.) quite a cheap hobby I think cos you just pay for some boots you literally pay a hundred quid a year and I just go and do it all the time

You might have noticed that it is Charlie's mum who introduces the topic of football, almost instructing him to talk about it, using it as a means to encourage her son to begin talking. This conversation demonstrates what social constructivists would call an interactive and negotiated construction of the son's gender. From the start the mother positions her son within the masculine stereotype of being interested in football by saying at the start, 'you can talk about football'.

In this section of the talk, the son is aware of his teenage identity and explicitly references this in the noun phrases 'generic little teenager' and 'typical teenager'. This self-positioning as a teenager first is also evident in his language use. His age (and perhaps gender) identity is also encoded into his speech style with the clipping of words like 'playin'' and 'an'', reflecting a non-standard use that suggests the boy gets some covert prestige with using such forms despite talking to his mother! This construction of himself as a teenager is evident too in his repetition of 'effort', a current clichéd term used by teenagers to show their annoyance at being asked to do anything.

4 Language and Gender

> **KEY TERMS**
>
> **Clipping:** the process of shortening words by not articulating some of the sounds, usually at the beginning or ends of words
>
> **Covert prestige:** the status and prestige gained from using a non-standard variety of English

4.3 Exploring identity and masculinities

When talking about football, Charlie presents his feelings about watching football but, more importantly to him, the playing of the game. In this, he seems to be aware of how he might be perceived by his male friends, disclosing to his mother in this private context how he tells his friend about winning but not the reason – playing a side with fewer players. He chooses to deliberately *exclude* this information as this would not construct an identity to his friend of him as a successful male.

His language choices construct gender, with references to *men* and *lads*, along with the plural pronoun *we* to refer to his team. This is what Raewyn Connell (1987) calls hegemonic masculinity as sports and competition are stereotypically connected with a representation of men as powerful and dominant. Here he may be calling upon his own knowledge that the language of football is dominated by these kinds of address terms and so he is calling upon a way of talking that is typical from being part of the community of practice (a concept we explored briefly in Chapter 1) seen in both amateur and professional football teams.

> **KEY TERM**
>
> **Hegemonic masculinity:** behaviours and language associated with the idealised male group that is seen as having the most power and status in society

When he expresses his 'urge' to play the game as a preference to watching football he is positioning himself to this version of masculinity in his talk. However, maybe as he is talking to his mother and not his friend he also uses adjectives like 'sad' and 'nice' to talk about his feelings about playing football, describing it as his 'hobby', constructing for her a softer version of the masculinity that he performs for his friends.

Gender and identity

Let's explore another section of the talk between Charlie and his mother in Text 4B. This looks at how he presents himself in a different way as the topic shifts to his upcoming prom, a dance held for students to celebrate the end of school after their GSCE exams.

Text 4B

Charlie: no we've still got quite a bit to get I think it's worth it though cos I love that suit it looks like so dapper [*Mum laughs*] that's how I like to put it to Paige it is it just looks so good

Mum: have you had a look yet at shirts and things

Charlie: er no not really (.) I need t' sort it out (.) but I need to see how long the sale (.) carries on for for at House Of Frazer (.) everyone's so buzzin' for it though everyone's just talking about it right now tryin' to sort everything out cos obviously there's after prom we got to sort that out an' I've not even sorted out getting there (.) don't know what we're going to do (2.0) do'y know what I was um I was speaking to Oscar cos he cos his mum got him a watch for prom an I said he can have my fake Armani one [*laughing*] it was free wasn't it (.) so he can just have it and I thought it was better but then we'll be turning up in our suits already look similar and we'll have the same watches and me and Oscar just on photos it'll look just so bad it'll be cute [*mum laughs*] he's my prom date

In many ways here, Charlie calls upon some of the language choices that Robin Lakoff (one of the main gender researchers in the 'dominance' approach that you read about in Chapter 1) found associated with women. He uses qualifiers like 'I think' and intensifiers like 'so dapper' and 'so good'. However, he could be calling upon these subconsciously to position himself in relation to the women he interacts with, calling upon this softened masculinity to appeal to them. His mother's laughter at him calling himself 'dapper' (meaning a man dressed fashionably) seems to show her approval and he has clearly already practised this phrase too on his female friend Paige. This feminine language is seen later in his selection of the (what Lakoff would term) empty adjective 'cute', another supposed example of female language to mock himself and his friend, who he jokingly refers to as his 'prom date'. He is actively presenting an identity that differs from his earlier positioning of himself as part of a hegemonic masculinity in his football talk, using a feminine language repertoire to almost present a gay identity, seemingly showing within one brief conversation how the representation of a 'gender' is complicated by other factors, for example his view of himself as a teenage male and the ways that he wants to be seen by others.

4.3.1 Constructing different masculinities and femininities

Throughout the book we have been challenging the notion that there is a feminine and masculine binary. We have just seen how Charlie, a teenage boy, has performed and constructed different versions of his masculine identity, so it seems relevant to discuss how femininity and masculinity might be constructed in more than one way as well as being associated with being powerful and powerless. Kate Bornstein (1998) views gender as a pyramid of power with some gendered identities at the top and others at the bottom. If we relate this to Connell's categories of masculinities, which we will look at shortly, it could look something like the Pyramid of power in Figure 4.1.

Figure 4.1: Pyramid of power

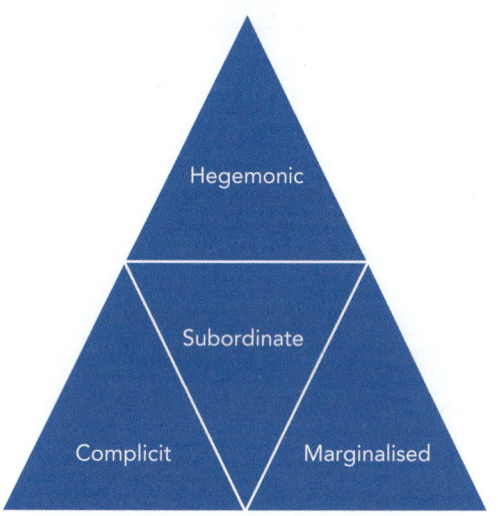

Applying this to Connell's models of masculinities, the most stereotypical version of masculinity, *hegemonic masculinity,* would be at the top of the pyramid. This would be because it's the masculinity associated with success in the workplace and in important public roles in society. It is also connected to the types of success that show men's physical and competitive power such as being an outstanding sportsman. Connell's three further types of masculinities are viewed as lesser forms to the all-powerful hegemonic one:

- **Subordinate masculinity**: showing qualities opposite to hegemonic and therefore viewed as weaker/inferior. This can often be seen in the negative labelling of men seen as subordinate as 'gay' or in the 'geek' or 'nerd' male; in other words those men who do not live up to the heterosexual stereotype of being assertive, strong and manly. We saw this in Chapter 3 where we

Gender and identity

investigated the media's negative representation of stay-at-home fathers as weak and not fulfilling masculine roles as successful professional men.

- **Complicit masculinity**: not fitting the masculinity criteria for hegemonic masculinity but a man who does not challenge it because they admire the qualities of men who have physical or social power.
- **Marginalised masculinity**: having masculinity that fits the characteristics of hegemonic masculinity but is excluded on the basis of other factors. These could be race or because they have some kind of physical disability.

In contrast, the hegemonic femininity associated with women is not about social power but instead depends on women's appearance and physical attractiveness. In fact, Connell does not use an equal term for masculinity, calling it emphasised femininity, immediately placing female identity as less powerful to men. You have only to think of the clichéd American school films featuring jocks (the successful football players and sportsmen of the school) and their equivalents (the cheerleaders) to recognise the power imbalance between these stereotyped masculine and feminine identities.

KEY TERM
Emphasised femininity: a complement to the hegemonic masculinity of men by accommodating the interests of men through feminine behaviours and attributes such as physical appearance

4.4 Identity and constructing selves through phonological choices

In a similar way to the continuing debate over Robin Lakoff's identification of tag questions as a female speech trait, debates over the differences in women's speech styles still seem to revert to the argument about whether women's language is powerless rather than powerful. It's not just words that can create a sense of power but the sounds of speech and there are two phonological areas of current interest to linguistic researchers: uptalk and the vocal fry.

KEY TERMS
Uptalk: also known as high rising terminal, it refers to where declarative statements end with rising intonation

Vocal fry: a vocal effect produced by the very slow vibration of the vocal cords and characterised by a creaking sound and low pitch

Language and Gender

4.4.1 Uptalk

One of the most recent social phenomena noticed in American English has been in young women's speech styles. Firstly this can be seen in what sociolinguistic researchers define as 'uptalk'. This is where a declarative sentence is produced with a rising intonation, making it sound more like a question. For example, 'I'm having a great day' would be produced in the way that it seems like a question: 'I'm having a great day?' It used to be called Valley Girl speak, taking its name from a popular song of the 1980s in America that made fun of young white Californian women's speech style of the time. Popular films of the time also parodied this stereotype of young women as unintelligent and slightly empty-headed. However, more recently linguists have found that this use of the rising inflection can actually have a variety of meanings in different situations and may not just be used by women.

Researchers from the University of California conducted an experiment with 23 young adult Southern Californians from contrasting backgrounds, including 11 men. Renaming uptalk 'SoCal English' (an abbreviation for the accent and dialect of Southern California) they found that both women and men use uptalk, although they still found some gender-based differences. Women used uptalk almost twice as often as men and women's rising intonation began later in a sentence and hit higher pitches. Yet, one key similarity was that when speakers were making a simple, declarative statement, men and women used rises with similar frequency. So, what did the researchers conclude from this? They saw the rising intonation as acting as a confirming statement, checking that the listener understood them. Adopting the uptalk strategy also allowed the speaker to hold the conversational floor as the rising intonation signalled to the listener that their conversational turn had not finished. In this study, women spoke with the floor-holding rise nearly 60 per cent of the time compared to men, who used it only 28 per cent of the time. One striking conclusion was that women may use uptalk as a defence mechanism against being interrupted.

KEY TERMS

Valley Girl speak: the colloquial dialect associated with Californian English and the associated stereotype of girls who use this

Hold the conversational floor: speak until you have finished what you wish to say or until someone interrupts you

4.4.2 Vocal fry

Vocal fry is where a speaker adopts a creaky low-pitch speech style and features a vibration that elongates some words. For example, with vocal fry a word like 'whatever' would be pronounced more like 'whateverrrrrr'. Some commentators have noticed that American women particularly use vocal fry. Like uptalk, there are both positive and negative interpretations associated with it. Because of its lower pitch, some people suggest that women are assuming it as a means of being taken more seriously in the workplace (perhaps because they sound more like a man) and part of their professional identity. In a contrary view, others believe that it gives young women a kind of stereotyped identity as slightly immature and lacking in intelligence.

For further reading, a 2012 article from the Science section of *The New York Times* titled 'They're, Like, Way Ahead of the Linguistic Currrrve' offers a comprehensive account of the rise of vocal fry and the linguistic research surrounding it. In this article, the authors cite the study that brought vocal fry to the attention of the public. In a small-scale study, researchers at Long Island University let participants listen to the same person (with both male and female speakers featured) say 'thank you for considering me for this opportunity', firstly in their normal speaking voice and then with a vocal fry. Participants were then asked to judge who was the most competent, educated, trustworthy, attractive and ultimately the most hireable for a job. Their conclusion was interesting too from a gender perspective as participants viewed female vocal fry speakers more negatively than men.

4.5 Occupational talk: conveying a gendered identity in the workplace

The workplace is now an important place to explore gender and so researchers have been keen to see if there are differences (or similarities) between men's and women's interactions and in their linguistic behaviours in a variety of workplace activities. These have ranged from studies into the language used by female and male employees in large call centres to the types of language used by women in more senior leadership roles in more formal settings like business meetings.

Judith Baxter's (2014) concept of double-voicing (drawn from the work of the Russian philosopher Mikhail Bakhtin) is interesting to apply to an exploration of gender identity in the workplace. She believes that as women are more aware than men that the people they are interacting with may have other agendas, they adjust their own language to reflect this knowledge. Here are some real examples from her research that she gives to illustrate how women double-voice:

- 'I realise I am being over-simplistic as usual but…'
- 'You have probably thought about this point already but…'

4 Language and Gender

- 'I have probably got my wires crossed but should we consider…?'
- 'I am no expert like the rest of you but…'

Baxter offers a number of categories to describe the various forms that double-voicing might take but significant here are two: anticipatory and mitigating.

- With *anticipatory* double-voicing a speaker demonstrates in their language that they have anticipated the response of others and attempts to dilute or deflect the criticism they expect.

- With *mitigating* double-voicing a speaker attempts to build solidarity and might also appear tentative and defensive. You can see how some of the ways that speakers double-voice may be marked by many of Lakoff's features of women's language.

Baxter's workplace research shows that women double-voice more than men and she concludes that women use this as a method of gaining approval.

KEY TERMS

Double-voicing: where speakers adjust their own language to reflect the agendas of the people with whom they are interacting

Anticipatory double-voicing: where the double-voicing anticipates and dilutes the criticism of others

Mitigating double-voicing: where the double-voicing offsets the distance, reduces authority and builds solidarity with a team

ACTIVITY 4.2

Investigating women's language in the workplace

In Text 4C a female teacher is speaking in her weekly department meeting about her new training role supporting teachers across the school. As you read the transcript, have in mind Robin Lakoff's list of the features of women's language:

- Hedging (with phrases like *sort of* and *it seems like*)
- Politeness strategies and apologies
- Tag questions
- Empty adjectives

Gender and identity

- Hypercorrect grammar and pronunciation
- Direct quotation
- Turning declarative statements into questions
- Using qualifiers (for example, 'I think that…')
- Modal constructions
- Indirect commands and requests and intensifiers (like 'so' and 'very').

1 Which ones can you identify the female speaker using in this single speaker discourse?
2 What do these suggest about women's language and the speaker's presentation of her identity?

Text 4C

Teacher: um (.) right well I'm supposed to introduce myself but I think you know who I am (.) um I've just come to let you know what's involved if you wanted to sign up (.) um how to do it (.) there are ten champions (.) you saw some of them in the advert last week (.) erm there's myself and Lesley [*she lists all the champions by name and subject*] (.) who you'd be working with would depend on what you were interested in and when you were willing to meet as well (.) so it wouldn't necessarily be just cos I've come to explain it today (.) wouldn't necessarily mean you're working with me or Lesley (.) um the idea is that we lead small (.) I'm leading small collaborative groups of volunteers and none of us is trying to claim to be experts in anything (.) we're just championing the cause of teaching and learning more that you know we're not kinda going in with all the ideas um you know (.) [*reading from the script*] ask them what he does is to stress that teaching staff here are very good most lessons are two (.) erm so we're not trying to (.) it's just rather than paying outside experts to come in it's about sharing good ideas within college (.) um so it's an opportunity to work with people from other departments and maybe get a fresh perspective and share ideas and good practice (.) um we're available to watch part of lessons if you want us to er (.) if you want to try something new and you want an outsider you want someone to come and watch a bit and give you feedback although that's not compulsory (.) you don't have to do that

Language and Gender

4.6 Social constructing self: performing gender in public and written contexts

We have already looked at a social constructivist approach to gender identity. However, an up-to-date view of gender is to combine this approach with a recognition that 'differences' might also exist. This is not a return to the 1970s difference approach but includes some of the ideas that we considered at the beginning of the chapter – that other aspects of identity might be important alongside gender. In a post-structuralist view of gender, diversity is seen as important as it pays attention to the interaction between factors such as class, ethnicity and gender. It also takes account of the fact that there are multiple presentations of masculinities and femininities, as well as individual differences among men and individual differences among women.

Part of this post-structuralist approach is Judith Butler's notion of gender continuously being performed (explored in Chapter 1), suggesting that people are aware of the language behaviours associated with masculine and feminine identities and make deliberate choices to reflect these. Associated with performativity is the idea that people have agency and can position themselves. We will explore this idea of women and men as having agency in the following activity that focuses on the performance of gender and as agents seeking romance.

> ### KEY TERMS
>
> **Post-structuralist:** a theory that rejects the notion of binary oppositions and sees that many perspectives exist rather than one fixed meaning
>
> **Agency:** a semantic concept where the agent (the doer of the action) is connected to the action expressed through the verb

> ### ACTIVITY 4.3
> **Investigating dating language and gender identity**
>
> Look at the examples of personal advertisements shown in Table 4.1. These would appear in British broadsheet newspapers like *The Guardian*. Ordinary people write these advertisements to try to find a partner for romance.
>
> These short advertisements are constrained by word limits and the writer has to choose their words carefully to both position and present

Gender and identity

themselves and to state their ideals in a partner in order to construct the identity of their perfect match. Thus the construction of identity is also in many ways interactive and negotiated as the personal advertisements are intended to be interpreted by a text receiver for a match and potential date.

- How do other identities interact with gender in these adverts?

- Create a list of the adjectives used by the women and men about themselves and the adjectives they use to describe the attributes they seek in a new partner. How do these construct masculine and feminine identities? In what ways are the writers 'performing' gender?

- Is there a difference between the language used by men and women to present themselves and to present the 'opposite' gender? What agency do the writers show? How do they use noun phrases to describe themselves and describe what they 'seek' from a partner?

To help you understand the initialisms commonly used in these types of advertisements, GSOH stands for *good sense of humour*, LTR means *long-term relationship*, WLTM indicates *would like to meet* and n/s refers to *no smoking*.

Table 4.1: Personal advertisements

Personal advertisements written by women	Personal advertisements written by men
Beautiful Blonde Saxophonist. Slovakian F, 40s, fit, intelligent, elegant, many interests. Seeks tall, professional, successful, M, 55–60, n/s with GSOH	**Almost Too Good To Be True.** Tall, charming, considerate & unassuming M, 47, various creative and active interests. Seeks a friendly, feminine lady for something serious.
Attractive, Professional brunette F, early 40s. Seeks handsome, sincere M for friendship.	**Sheffield Bloke, 44**, only looks 43. Can appear interesting on a date. Think John Lennon with a touch of Elvis thrown in and that's me.
Tall, Good-looking F, 62, loves cooking, ballroom dancing & spoiling people. Seeks good-looking, kind, sweet-natured M with a social conscience.	**Pink Floyd Fan** & History and Politics Loving Lecturer. Slim M, 71, in good state of health seeks r/ship with slim F. Together to make life fun.

4 Language and Gender

Personal advertisements written by women	Personal advertisements written by men
Brave Female Traveller. 61. Seeks anchor man who's warm, witty, loyal & open to new ideas.	**No Egos Here Please.** M, 55, medium build likes 70s music, the Costa Blanca & Barcelona. WLTM a slim, petite, happy-go-lucky, smiley F for straightforward, ego-free LTR.
Sincere, Slim, Attractive, stylish F, 46, charming, cultured & caring, of Asian origin with forward-thinking European outlook & SOH. Is there a warm, considerate, n/s M out there to warm the winter days?	**Grumpy Old Toad!** Ex Prince Charming, now dressed up as a warty old toad. Needs princess to kiss and release.

4.7 Performing and constructing gender identity in a modern world

Clearly in a world governed by social media and computer-mediated communication, identity can be presented in many ways and in a wide variety of genres: blogs, posts, direct messages, forums, tweets, and so on. At the beginning of the chapter you were asked to reflect on these in relation to yourself and your own constructed identity in these genres and text types. In these hybrid online modes, we communicate with a wide range of different communities and groups: family, friends, colleagues, people we share interests with, and so on. In all these, we use language and other features that either express or construct the identities that we want to present. Another consideration that we might make as we communicate in a computer-mediated context is whether these are public or private.

Text 4D shows an exchange from a family WhatsApp group – a private group limited to close family members. As you read, note the gender identities that are being presented in this family exchange between a father and his 21-year-old daughter. Think about how they are 'doing' gender and making it an explicit part of their interaction, in addition to the more subtle presentations of feminine and masculine behaviours.

Text 4D

What you might have picked up on is the function of the exchanges and how this links to gender identity. With the topic of the internet not working (Virgin is the name of a British internet provider), Izzy addresses her father but shifts topic when this is sorted to granny's phone call and directly addresses her mother. The stereotype of men as more technical and women as more interested in interactional and social relationships seems confirmed here by the daughter's directing of her communication within the family group chat by requesting her father's assistance. Gendered address terms, such as 'mr father' and 'miss daughter' are used, although perhaps in a humorous mocking way as Izzy's 'mr' may just be a typo of 'my' and her dad responds to this by playing on the female term. Yet Izzy's later address to her father as 'boss' reaffirms her view of him as in control of the technology. The father's response to Izzy's interrogative is also imperative, instructing Izzy with the verbs 'switch' and 'start', and is elliptical in style.

4 Language and Gender

> **RESEARCH QUESTION**
> **Identity in the workplace**
>
> You could take any of the central ideas discussed in this chapter and conduct more research. For example, there has been much recent research into gendered identity in the workplace and you could explore further studies and their findings through wider reading (such as the texts listed at the end of this chapter) and reflect on your own experiences in a workplace.
>
> Using a search engine like Google Books or Google Scholar, you can use key words to find information on research by people such as Janet Holmes, Marie Stubbe, Judith Baxter and Sara Mills.

4.8 Conclusion

In this chapter, you have explored a variety of interactional situations where gender can be performed, constructed or expressed. These demonstrate the flexible nature of our identities as we move in and out of different interactional settings. With today's communication methods, we can perhaps even manage these identities simultaneously – interacting with others in the 'real' world at the same time as in the 'virtual' world so often now contained on our smartphones or via computer-mediated communication. What we haven't focused on so much is the larger picture of male and female identity within very high-profile and public contexts; for example, in areas such as politics and high-level leadership roles in corporations. In these settings ideas about what is masculine and feminine behaviour might impact both the ways that women and men present themselves and how other people make judgements about them based on expectations based around their gender. This is something that you may want to return to once you have explored some key research methods in the next chapter.

Wider reading

You can find out more about the concepts and ideas in this chapter by reading these books:

Connell, R.W. (2005) *Masculinities* (Second edition). Cambridge: Polity Press.

Eckert, P. and McConnell-Ginet, S. (2013) *Language and Gender* (Second edition). Cambridge: Cambridge University Press.

Holmes, J. (2006) *Gendered Talk at Work: Constructing Gender Identity Through Workplace Discourse*. Oxford: Blackwell.

Chapter 5
Exploring gender: applying research methods to data

In this chapter you will:

- Learn about different research methods
- Explore how theories about gender can be applied to data
- Develop your own research skills

5 Language and Gender

5.1 Introduction

In the opening chapter, we explored the history of gender studies from the beginning of the twentieth century to the present day. From this historical perspective, we saw how views and theories about language and gender have changed greatly over time. We then focused on specific aspects relevant to gender study:

- How English as a language both *uses* and *constructs* gender in various grammatical and lexical and semantic ways

- The ways that gender is *represented* in a variety of text types

- Issues associated with gender and *identity*.

Now it's time for you to become an active researcher into those areas of language and gender that have particularly interested you. In this chapter, we'll consider the stages of writing a research project: from your first ideas and writing focused research questions, to collecting suitable data, to deciding on the right method of analysis and the importance of reading around your chosen topic area. In research projects, we often use the term 'data' to refer to the texts or other material (such as interviews or questionnaires) that we generate.

ACTIVITY 5.1

Beginning your investigation

A starting point for any research project is to find out what interests you most about the topic. Any linguistic research project will involve you studying your chosen topic and data over quite a long period of time, so it needs to keep your interest.

As a first step, go back through the previous chapters and note down information about the following:

- The types of texts and data that we have explored. (For example, we have looked at a range of spontaneous spoken data and advertisements and headlines from newspaper articles.)

- Methods and 'tools' used to research gender. (For example, we have seen how gender researchers have analysed conversation, conducted interviews and used corpora.)

Exploring gender: applying research methods to data

Next, write down your first ideas for what you'd like to explore. If you need help to focus your initial thoughts, see if the following statements apply to you:

- I am interested in how the media represents gender and gender stereotypes.
- I am interested in the ways that men and/or women talk.
- I am interested in how gender is represented in literature.
- I am interested in how gendered patterns can be seen in language use.

5.2 Creating your own research project

Here's an outline of the stages you will go through, even before you begin writing up your findings. You will:

1. Identify your broad area, question or hypothesis. (A hypothesis is a prediction about what you think you might find or a possible explanation that you want to study further.)
2. Choose what data/texts you want to collect and where you can get these from.
3. Decide what method(s) of data collection that you want to use.
4. Collect your data, allowing time to gather and collate it. Remember transcribing spoken data can take a long time, so you need to build this into your plan.
5. Read about your topic area to select the theories and studies that are relevant to your own research.

> **KEY TERM**
>
> **Hypothesis:** a question or prediction used as a starting point for further investigation

In thinking about your ideas, you may have identified your potential research area into language and gender, although you will need to narrow it down. Refining your focus will help you to select the right data and texts. To help guide you, you were

5 Language and Gender

given some statements and we can now use these to model how you can start narrowing down your idea. Saying 'yes' to the first statement, 'I am interested in how the media represents gender and gender stereotypes', only gives you a very broad focus on gender, stereotypes and the media. You should now start to ask yourself questions to give you a clearer steer towards stage 2 (data collection) and stage 3 (methods of data collection). Here are some examples of questions:

- Will I look at males or females?
- What are the stereotypes I might look for?
- What type of media (newspapers, advertisements, television, radio, etc.)?
- Do I want to explore if gender stereotypes are being broken down or if they have changed over time?

Now you can move to the next stages. But it's important that even once you have completed stages 1–5, you should go back to your overall research question. Ask yourself whether you need to change it and if your data is right for your question. If it's not, then you need to decide what is going to be better data to use and how to obtain it. At this point you are ready to begin analysing your data.

5.2.1 Deciding a focus: student case studies

To help guide you in your own research, we are going to look at some case studies of students who have chosen to do gender-based research projects. Table 5.1 outlines the gender topics that they have selected and the data and texts that they are using to help them to investigate their topics. As you read them, think about the hypothesis and/or angle on gender that they have selected. Look at their data. Ask yourself whether they have chosen the right data and if you can think of other types of data that they could have used.

Table 5.1: Summaries of student research areas and data choices

	Focus	Data/text types
Lily	Is there a difference in the language used by a male and female parent?	Computer-mediated communication: a selection of WhatsApp, Twitter, Facebook and text messages
Mia	An exploration into the language used by interviewers when interviewing male and female celebrities.	Transcripts from British and American chat shows

Exploring gender: applying research methods to data

	Focus	Data/text types
	Mia's hypothesis is that the interviewers will ask different questions and introduce different topics to talk about depending on whether the person being interviewed is male or female	
Ayesha	She is interested in her own language use. She has two initial research questions: • whether she changes her style in different situations • whether gender is a factor in her self-presentation.	Emails Transcripts Social media interactions
Ben	How advertisers promote health and beauty products to men and women and what stereotypes they use.	Advertisements Websites: health magazines for men and women and advertisers' websites A corpus created from perfume and aftershave names
Amy	Whether the representations of women have changed in literary texts, comparing and contrasting between female characters in novels from different time periods	Jane Austen's *Pride and Prejudice* and Helen Fielding's *Bridget Jones' Diary*. Advice texts on relationships from the nineteenth century and websites offering relationship advice

5.2.2 Choosing data types

You have probably seen from the case studies that choosing what data you will use is one of the most important parts of research. When considering whether to use data such as transcripts or text messages from yourself or from family members, you might need to factor in whether you are native English speakers or whether English is an additional language.

Throughout the book we have analysed a number of transcripts and, given the number of linguists who have focused their studies on exploring gender in spoken interactions, this seems a good place to start. In earlier chapters, we have looked at a range of spoken data. In Chapter 4, we explored a teenage

5 Language and Gender

boy's interaction with his mother. Although this was an example of spontaneous speech, it also occurred as the mother was interviewing her son for a research project. From this, you could consider how interviews and spontaneous speech can be used to investigate issues such as gender.

However, if you want to find out about people's attitudes towards gender and language, then you might want to create a questionnaire. Designing a clear questionnaire can be quite a challenge, so you should first research what makes a good questionnaire. Some features you might want to consider when writing your questions are:

- Are your questions clear?
- Are you going to ask respondents to tick option boxes?
- Do you want respondents to write their own responses?
- How many questions do you want to answer?
- What do you want to find out and what questions will help you achieve this?

There are free websites that you can use to create questionnaires. Creating one online also means that you could use social media or forums to post it and to gather your responses.

For written data, we have explored ways of looking at discourses and there are plenty of different types of texts that you can use to generate your data. We have focused on media and online sources to introduce issues surrounding the representation of gender and identity, but Ayesha's collection of data shows that you can find other written texts, for example letters, emails and notes. Ayesha also used minutes from her college Student Council meetings to see if she demonstrated typical features of female language or 'performed' in a different way in this more official and serious context.

You can also use blended mode data. Some ways that we communicate now (by using our phones or computers) are seen as a kind of talk and are examples of blended mode. Text messaging, WhatsApp and Facebook, amongst others, all include interactional features that we would associate with speech. This is because they are structured around turn-taking although the nature of replying to messages means that some aspects of speech (like overlaps) are not as evident.

For example, Text 5A, a text message conversation between a grandmother and her granddaughter, is structured into adjacency pairs. With this type of messaging, references to the time sent can also show how synchronous and like a real face-to-face conversation it can be.

Exploring gender: applying research methods to data

> **KEY TERMS**
>
> **Blended mode:** a text which contains conventional elements of both speech and writing
>
> **Overlaps:** when one speaker talks at the same time as another
>
> **Adjacency pairs:** a simple structure of two turns
>
> **Synchronous:** interaction that takes place in real time

Text 5A

5.2.3 Linking data to analytical approaches and methods

By choosing to focus on a particular group of people, you might draw on some of the investigation approaches used by researchers that we looked at earlier in this book. Here are some useful ones:

- **Ethnography:** This involves you *observing* your participants' talk in addition to *speaking* to the participants. You might conduct formal interviews where you ask them specific questions and record their answers. With this approach you are both 'outside' the culture you are investigating because you are not

5 Language and Gender

a participant in it yourself but are 'inside' it too because you get to know it really well whilst you are studying it. For this you would need regular contact with the group (or groups) of people that you want to investigate.

- **Communities of practice:** A concept that looks at the ways that groups of people often build up shared repertoires (i.e. shared ways of doing and saying things) when they come together. In the opening chapter, we briefly looked at some studies that found gendered behaviours in different social groups. You too could gather data on a group (or groups) – either in single-sex groups or as mixed groups who come together for a particular purpose – and investigate their ways of interacting and using language.

- **Critical Discourse Analysis (CDA):** An approach to discourse analysis for written and spoken texts that focuses on power and the ways that ideology can be conveyed in language. CDA researchers often focus on institutions like workplaces or public discourse such as politics, as well as how the media convey ideologies. You can see how you could find the emphasis on power useful when exploring language and gender. In one of our students' case studies, Mia was looking at interviewers' questioning of women on well-known popular chat shows. For her, analysing the power relationships between interviewer/interviewee and cultural and gendered ideologies associated with female actors might be really useful.

- **Stylistics:** An approach to studying literary and non-fiction texts (novels, drama and poetry) that gives detailed attention to the actual language being used. This means that you analyse and interpret the features and patterns you can see in the texts through accurately identifying them using precise linguistic terminology. You could apply the techniques of stylistics, like Amy in our earlier case study, to novels, or to explore particular discourses (ways of presenting people or ideas) in written texts aimed at men and women – just like Ben might do in his exploration of health websites aimed at men and women.

> **KEY TERM**
>
> **Stylistics:** the study of texts both focusing carefully on language and providing a rich interpretation of key concerns, themes and possible effects

5.2.4 Using methods: a corpus linguistics research project

So, what is corpus linguistics? Firstly, we need to think of this in a more general sense. Coming from the Latin, *corpus* means 'body'. When linguists talk about *corpora* (the plural of *corpus*), they are simply referring to collections of language data. However, a corpus has a much more specialised meaning.

Exploring gender: applying research methods to data

A corpus refers to a collection of language data that has been put together deliberately as an authentic and real sample of the language being used by speakers and writers. It can contain both spoken and written data and it can be created from a variety of sources – such as newspapers, real speech, emails and books. In order to be an effective tool to use to analyse language, a corpus aims to be as representative as possible, taking examples of language use in different modes and mediums of communication. Once a corpus has been created, linguists can use it to search for patterns or changes in language use.

Above all, corpus linguistics is about the systematic study of language. At one level, it allows you to quantify patterns by looking at statistical information. This statistical information is provided once you have requested the information you want the corpus to search. This is helpful if you don't have a mathematical background. More than this, it also gives you either words or lines of text to look at from which you can investigate the actual language content.

However, a good researcher will go below the surface of the numbers and add in qualitative interpretations to explain what the data seems to show about the ways that language is really being used. Corpus designers have created many search tools that you can use very easily. One of these is Sketch Engine, which processes individual words from corpora to find patterns of use. Within this search function, a word sketch can find collocations – words that seem to go together frequently and naturally like *pretty woman* or *handsome man* and something we looked at in Chapter 2. Word Sketch difference can search for two words and compare them to see what differences there are in their usage.

KEY TERMS

Corpus linguistics: the study of language based on real-life examples collected together within a corpus

Corpus: a collection of texts brought together with the purpose of study

Sketch Engine: a corpus tool to search language corpora

Word Sketch difference: an online search tool used to compare and contrast two words by analysing their collocations and by displaying the collocates divided into categories based on grammatical relations

ACTIVITY 5.2
Word Sketch difference

To see how you can use your interpretative skills on corpus data, we'll use the Word Sketch difference tool on The Cambridge Corpus for you to practise on. Here we are looking for differences (or similarities) in

5 Language and Gender

the collocations with *man/woman*. Table 5.2 contains the findings. The results show what words are either commonly used in *and/or* patterns such as man *and* woman and man *or* woman, or as adjectives.

Your task is to identify patterns and draw conclusions about the differences in collocations occurring with *man* and *woman* from this evidence.

- For *and/or* collocations in Table 5.2, what do you notice about the words most associated with each gender? For example, you could focus on the ways that age collocates with *woman* and see what is similar or different with *man*.

- In what semantic field can you place the *adjectives* most naturally collocating with woman in Table 5.2? What seems unusual but interesting about the amount of white, green and red in the table? (There are some explanations of what each colour means underneath the table to help you.)

Table 5.2: Word Sketch results for *man/woman*

and/or	22944	27724	1.8	1.5	adj_subject_of	3098	4773	2.6	2.8
officer	77	0	6.6	–	mortal	20	0	7.7	–
god	69	0	6.6	–	unemployed	17	8	7.3	5.7
mouse	66	0	6.3	–	alive	20	11	7.1	5.8
animal	317	10	8.4	3.2	capable	64	34	7.8	6.7
woman	10498	678	12.7	8.6	happy	21	17	7.4	6.6
masculinity	125	10	7.4	3.5	afraid	15	13	7.2	6.4
lesbian	113	10	7.3	3.5	responsible	75	70	7.6	7.3
nature	138	21	6.9	4.0	willing	48	53	8.0	7.8
world	84	20	6.5	4.2	aware	29	38	7.1	7.2
boy	204	68	7.9	6.1	able	106	160	7.6	8.0
wife	128	58	7.2	5.9	unable	21	40	6.7	7.3
%	189	188	6.6	6.5	more	35	68	6.4	7.2
work	72	144	5.8	6.6	active	34	79	7.5	8.3
example	104	205	5.6	6.5	likely	285	717	8.0	9.3
people	78	201	5.9	7.1	young	18	63	6.9	8.3
group	71	179	5.4	6.6	vulnerable	10	56	6.1	8.2
worker	29	90	4.9	6.3	subordinate	0	23	–	7.2
family	63	194	5.6	7.1	married	0	23	–	7.2
youth	17	84	4.5	6.5	single	0	24	–	7.2
widow	9	99	3.6	6.8	eligible	0	28	–	7.4
girl	32	376	5.2	8.6	unmarried	0	25	–	7.4
child	118	1459	6.0	9.5	ill	0	27	–	7.4
minority	9	179	3.6	7.6	religious	0	29	–	7.6
man	570	10498	8.7	12.7	disadvantaged	0	29	–	7.6
gender	0	143	–	6.7	pregnant	0	66	–	8.7

86

Exploring gender: applying research methods to data

You'll see from Table 5.2 that three colours are used: red, green and white.

- Collocates in **red** tend to combine with our red word *woman*.
- Collocates in **green** tend to combine with our green word *man*.
- **White** shows that this word combines with both *woman* and *man*.
- **Bolder** colours show a stronger collocation. To help you understand what this means, look at the table on the right where it shows what adjectives commonly go with *man/woman*. This table shows that it is more usual to say *mortal man* than *mortal woman* (the second column on the left shows this). On the other hand, it is more natural (if not surprising) to say *pregnant woman* than *pregnant man* (look at the number in the third column).

A corpus doesn't have to be just available in electronic form, so you can create your own corpora from data you collect. Indeed, this is what some of the students that we have looked at in the case studies have done.

RESEARCH QUESTION

A corpus linguistics investigation

You can access some excellent free online tools to help you carry out a corpus linguistics investigation. Here are some suggestions for you. Use these to practise your investigation skills. You can try out your own searches for key words and phrases relevant to researching gender.

- If you want to research language and gender in fiction, you can use CLiC, a corpus tool designed to help analyse literary texts. It's available at www.cambridge.org/links/escgen6005 and is the result of a collaboration between the University of Nottingham and the University of Birmingham. You can search how particular words or phrases are used in some of Charles Dickens' famous novels, as well as other selected nineteenth-century novels. Applying this to language and gender research, you could see how male and female fictional characters are presented.

Google's ngram viewer is available at www.cambridge.org/links/escgen6006. An ngram is a sequence of one or more words. Using Google Books, ngram viewer allows you to use their corpus of published works. Clearly there are limitations but you can search to see if a word, or a sequence of words, is being used more or less frequently over time. Figure 5.1 shows an example of a search for the adjective 'handsome' and noun 'woman' being used in a sequence. What conclusions can you draw about the use of this noun phrase over time?

5 Language and Gender

Figure 5.1: ngram for *handsome* and *woman*

5.3 Finding spoken data

The Listening Project is a joint project between the BBC and The British Library, who have recorded ordinary people (usually family and friends) speaking about particular topics of personal interest to them. These topics can be general, for example friendship, or falling in love or about things that are really important to the speakers such as illnesses and coping with difficult personal experiences. People who want to take part visit special recording places in regional radio stations. This project was based on an American one, *StoryCorps*, and this website (https://storycorps.org/) can also give you the opportunity to obtain spoken data from English speakers. Both the UK and US versions give a summary of the topic of each conversation so you can select ones that:

- feature single-gender or mixed-gender speakers
- are about a gendered topic
- focus on a particular gender identity or role.

YouTube is also a source of transcripts, as are radio and television. There are also many media websites that you can access to gather useful data.

Part of your decision-making involves considering the types of talk you can focus on. Here are some suggestions:

- Everyday speech that takes place in people's homes as part of family life – between parents and children, siblings, the extended family (grandparents, uncles, aunts, cousins)
- Public talk – where people like politicians are giving speeches or celebrities are being interviewed on talk shows
- Workplace talk – in organisations as part of people's work life

Exploring gender: applying research methods to data

5.3.1 Being an ethical researcher

How you collect your data is very important, especially if you are going to use 'real' people. You cannot just record people without their knowledge and you must get their consent to being recorded and to using their data. The most ethical way is to gain their permission quite formally by requesting this in writing. Often people are curious about why you are recording them but this can create problems for you as a researcher. For example, telling them that you are investigating whether gender affects language use might influence them so that they use language and 'perform' in very unusual ways. This is the observer's paradox, and was coined by William Labov (1972) to refer to the changes that can happen to people's speech style if they know that they are being recorded.

It's also important that you make sure that individual speakers can't be identified in the transcripts that you produce. You should make them anonymous by not using their real names. You can either choose another name for them, or you can label them as Speaker A, Speaker B, and so on. However, as you are focusing on investigating gender, it will be important to know the gender of every speaker in your transcript. One option is to label them using a code such as M1/M2 (or Male 1/Male 2) and F1/F2 for female participants.

> **KEY TERM**
>
> **Observer's paradox:** the issue of speakers being aware they are being recorded and the potential problems this may incur

5.4 Analysing conversations and making transcripts

When transcribing speech, you need to decide what is important to record in the final transcript. So it might be useful to have a broad idea of what you might be looking for. This will help you decide if you are interested in prosodic or paralinguistic features as well as the words that the participants use. Looking back at the transcripts featured in this book, or in others in the series, will help you identify what aspects of conversations you want to present in the final transcript.

You can use Conversation Analysis (CA) as a method to explore people taking part in conversations and see whether this shows a difference between women and men. In Conversation Analysis, researchers' main focus is on the ways that

Language and Gender

people organise their conversations and here you would analyse the patterns that you can see in the following areas:

- turn-taking: how turns are arranged

- turn allocation: who gets to speak.

There are some cultural factors that you might also need to consider to explore turn-taking used by native English speakers. In general, there is the assumption that interrupting someone is considered rude and that there are turn transition relevance places marking where a new speaker can take a turn. The speaker might show that they are ready to give up a turn in a variety of ways. They could show this through prosodic features like a falling intonation on their words to show that they have finished. Also a rising intonation can indicate that the speaker has asked a question that needs a new speaker to respond. Speakers use many non-verbal cues such as eye contact or gestures to show either that they have finished speaking or that they want someone else to speak. But a speaker can also signal that they have finished what they have said grammatically so that the hearer would know that what they have said is complete. To illustrate this, look at Text 5B, taken from another part of the transcript between Charlie, the teenage boy featured in Chapter 4, and his mother. In this Charlie's mother uses Charlie's tag questions as a cue to speak.

> ### KEY TERMS
>
> **Prosodic features:** aspects of intonation, speed and volume
>
> **Paralinguistic features:** aspects of spoken language that do not involve words
>
> **Conversation Analysis:** an approach to the study of conversation in everyday interactions
>
> **Turn-taking:** the process by which speakers co-construct conversation
>
> **Turn allocation:** the process by which turns are managed in interactions
>
> **Turn transition relevance place:** a point where it is natural for another speaker to take a turn
>
> **Tag question:** a short question used at the end of a sentence, often inviting agreement with the speaker

Exploring gender: applying research methods to data

Text 5B

Charlie: I mainly listen to house music but you an dad complain about it (.) that's what I did what you guys were out (2) then grime's just lyrical isn't it (.) it's like rap but it's not really listened to is it

Mum: what do you mean about not really listen to

Charlie: it's like low on the UK scene isn't it (.) no one listens to it really (.) people my age that's is (.) and all the people from your school by the sounds of things (.) it never really goes off (.) it was on Channel 4 news you know

Mum: was it

When any of the cues we have highlighted happen, turn allocation can take place. A speaker can make it clear who should speak next by allocating a turn to someone else, or another speaker can self-select and take his or her turn. Clearly, this makes conversation seem very neat but there are times when speakers can overlap and speak at the same time as someone else – often called simultaneous speech. This might be a simple mistake; they had thought the other person had finished their turn. It could also occur because the listener wants to show that they are interested in what the speaker has said. However, if the listener does this deliberately with the purpose of taking the turn away then this is an interruption.

KEY TERMS

Simultaneous speech: where speakers talk at the same time as each other

Interruption: the action of speaking at the same time as another speaker with the intention of taking the turn from them

Sometimes key information about the context of the talk will be important in helping you to interpret your data. Making a list of contextual information about the speakers will be very useful. Apart from their gender, this list might include the speakers' ages, their ethnic background and their occupation but you might also think of other 'identities' that you could note down. Apart from more detail about the individual participants, other factors such as where the interaction took place might be relevant to your analysis. The conversation might have taken place in a school, or in a shop, or in a bus queue and these different locations could affect the type of language that the speakers use and how they interact with each other.

5 Language and Gender

5.4.1 Analysing conversations and gender

So, how does this apply to exploring gender? We have already looked in the first chapter at how some theorists have used transcripts of naturally occurring speech between single-sex or mixed-sex participants and drawn conclusions about how men and women use language differently.

One research option available to you is to replicate a study that's been done before and test out whether their findings still hold true today. Don Zimmerman and Candace West's famous 'dominance' study in 1975 found that men interrupted women more in mixed-sex conversation. Recording conversations at the University of California, they found that men interrupted 46 times in 11 conversations between women and men (96 per cent of the time). From this they concluded that men are more dominant in conversations that also feature women. They used this as evidence of men's power in society generally. Zimmerman and West's study was at the time when researchers adopted a dominance approach to investigating language and gender. Of course, being open-minded is important in research and an interruption by itself may not show dominance by one party over another. Later researchers have been critical of this study and how its findings were generalised to include all men and women. One of the criticisms centred on what classed as an interruption and whether this was always a sign of dominance. For example, in a later study that Zimmerman and West did, a man 'interrupted' his female conversational partner because she was 'leafin through' his notebook whilst she was talking and he used the imperative 'don't touch that' to tell her to stop. This highlights how important it is to recognise and understand the contexts of speakers' utterances. You too might not like someone else touching your study notes and think that he's being perfectly reasonable in his request, rather than just showing his dominance over the female participant.

We can apply this need for open-mindedness to some data. In one of our student case studies, Lily was exploring her parents' use of language and applying the 'difference' model. Looking at the Twitter messages in Text 5C, it seems that Lily could prove this point.

Text 5C

Lily's mum

Lily's dad

Exploring gender: applying research methods to data

And yet, in another set of Lily's data, we can see something entirely different. Text 5D shows WhatsApp messages sent to her by her parents. These suggest other interpretations. As you read them, think about how these messages, particularly the one from Lily's dad, demonstrate the performative and constructed aspects of gender, and are examples of Lily's family having their own familylect (particular words and phrases used as a private language between family members) or community of practice.

Text 5D

5.5 Reading about language and gender

Throughout this book there have been suggestions for further reading to develop your knowledge and understanding further. These were based initially on the key theories of 'dominance', 'difference', 'deficit' and 'diversity'. In later chapters, the wider reading was linked to some of the ideas that we explored. You can use these lists to help you read around your chosen topic. But information is not just available in books. Many linguistic researchers share their ideas on academic websites such as academia.edu or on their university pages. Twitter is another useful resource to find people posting links to newspaper articles and recent research.

5 Language and Gender

Because gender is a very popular topic to study in linguistics there are also many helpful blogs that collect relevant resources to help you to understand the key ideas and concepts associated with language and gender. You could look at this blog, available at www.cambridge.org/links/escgen6007, which collects resources.

There are also websites and blogs written by academics but aimed at your level of understanding. These summarise linguistic research into a variety of topics but in a very accessible and clear manner. Try exploring www.cambridge.org/links/escgen6008 for short summaries of research into gender topics. Another similar website is available at www.cambridge.org/links/escgen6009. Even some well-known gender theorists have their own blogs. One of these is Deborah Cameron, whose ideas you were introduced to earlier. As well as writing books like *The Myth of Mars and Venus*, she shares her views about language and gender on her blog: www.cambridge.org/links/escgen6010.

Why is it so important to do secondary reading? In any academic research, relating your findings to what other researchers have found or think is crucial to make your own analysis valid. You might find areas that challenge others' beliefs and this is good too. We have challenged some of the theories as we have gone through and you have seen that approaches to language and gender study have changed over time.

5.6 Acknowledging your sources

Making sure that you acknowledge who and what you have read is another really important element of research. This will show your reader that you have taken your project seriously and have come to reasoned and logical conclusions based on a sound understanding of the topic. As you read, make sure you keep a record of the following:

- Who – the author(s)

- What – the name of the text

- When – date

- Where – more details of the source such as the hyperlink if it's from a website.

Producing a list of references and a bibliography is essential. Most universities offer guides to referencing but there are also online referencing tools that are simple to use. Harvard referencing is the most commonly used system and it is worth becoming familiar with this.

Exploring gender: applying research methods to data

ACTIVITY 5.3
Reading about and researching gender theories

- Use the links to websites and blogs from the 'reading about language and gender' section. Search for gender-related topics within these. Read a selection and note down interesting points about gender and language. Go back to your first ideas and see if these are useful to your own investigation or if they give you new ideas either for research topics or for linguistic features to explore.

- Search for information and advice on using Harvard referencing and online referencing tools. Practise using these by typing in the details for one of the books listed in 'Wider reading' at the end of the chapter.

5.7 Practising decision-making

Throughout this chapter, we have considered the stages of designing and developing a research project into gender. As a final task, look at Text 5E, which shows some text messages for you to practise your decision-making and research skills. Data set 1 is text messages between two male friends, aged 18. Data set 2 is text messages between two female friends, aged 18. When you have read Text 5E, answer the Practice question.

PRACTICE QUESTION
Data sets 1 and 2

- What research questions or hypotheses can you suggest for the data?
- What gender theories are you going to 'test'? Think about which ones would be most relevant for the data. Start with the big categories of 'dominance', 'difference', 'deficit', 'diversity' and 'performance'. Which of these aren't going to be useful?

Now look at the data more carefully:

- What else apart from gender could be relevant contextually to the data?
- What linguistic features do you notice? Annotate the texts for specific lexical/semantic, grammatical or discourse features.
- How do these prove or disprove your hypothesis or research question?

Finally, think about what you can do next to research language and gender and use the skills gained from this 'mini' research task.

5 Language and Gender

Text 5E

Data set 1

Data set 2

5.8 Conclusion

So why study language and gender? The answer is because it is part of the English language itself – both in its grammar and in the ways that words and their connotations encapsulate social attitudes and our sense of our own identity. Gender researchers, both past and present, have also helped us to question how the English language can change and evolve as we change as societies. In a sense, this has only been the beginning of your study of gender. By touching on key issues and concepts and introducing you to the theorists, you can now be aware of gender and the ways we talk about and represent it on a daily basis.

Wider reading

You can find out more about the concepts and ideas in this chapter by reading these books:

Fairclough, N. (2014) *Language and Power* (Third edition). London: Routledge.

McEnery, T. and Wilson, A. (2001) *Corpus Linguistics* (Second edition). Edinburgh: Edinburgh University Press.

Simpson, P. (2014) *Stylistics: A Resource Book for Students* (Second edition). London: Routledge.

Wray, A. and Bloomer, A. (2013) *Projects in Linguistics and Language Studies* (Third edition). Abingdon: Routledge.

Ideas and answers

Chapter 1

Activity 1.1

If you tested out folk linguistics (ordinary people's beliefs about language), reflect on your findings. If people tended to agree with the statements, you might have been surprised – or not – by their beliefs about language and gender. Folk linguistics is interesting because it assesses what society believes is true about language use and you might start thinking about the potential effects of this.

You might also want to reflect on the method that you used for data gathering. Think about the advantages and disadvantages of the method that you chose. When you read Chapter 5, you will be making choices about investigation approaches and the ways that you can collect data. Having practised these here, you'll be in a good position to understand how to conduct primary research (interviews, questionnaires, speech recordings).

Asking people to write down their responses	Could you control their responses? Did they write as much as you wanted them to?
Recording people and transcribing their feedback	Was this easy to manage? What recording equipment did you use? How easy or difficult was it to transcribe? How much time did it take you?
Interviewing people	Were people happy to give up their time for an interview? Did you think your questions were effective?

Activity 1.2

This task showed you how you can use previous linguistic studies as a basis for your own investigations. We are going to look at this further as a valid research method in Chapter 5. As Robin Lakoff conducted her research in the 1970s you might have found that:

- Difference still exists between women's use of a special colour lexicon and men's.
- The difference is less pronounced than Lakoff's assertion – that men did use some more precise labelling of colours.
- It depends on the individual and that gender is not a significant factor.

Ideas and answers

Activity 1.3

Non-standard forms are fairly common occurrences in song lyrics, for popular songs and some more specific musical genres such as rap. Many singers sing in an American accent, so the phonological clipping of words to the 'n' sound might be a response to this real or assumed accent. If you looked at a more recent musical genre like the UK's Grime, many of the artists reflect more recognisable urban English accents (London, Manchester or Birmingham) and these are likely to show the dropping of the 'g'. Much of the sociolinguistic research found that other factors such as age or social background were important too and you may have drawn similar conclusions. The dropping of the 'g' is often a feature of teen sociolect, the style of language adopted by younger English speakers. So, other aspects apart from our gender may influence our language choices and this will be a discussion in Chapter 4.

Chapter 2

Activity 2.1

What different semantic fields did you think of? The suggestions offered were these ones, but you might have thought of others:

- Emotions (airhead, ditsy, hormonal, emotional, hysterical, illogical)

- Appearance (bombshell, curvy, voluptuous, frumpy)

- Behaviours (high-maintenance, sassy, ambitious, bossy, abrasive, bitchy, Bridezilla, frigid, bolshy, bubbly, pushy, whinging)

Words with emotional connotations seem to present women as not in control of themselves ('hormonal', 'hysterical') or as lacking in brain power ('airhead', 'illogical'). With appearance, judgements are positive on traditionally feminine shapes ('curvy', 'voluptuous') and negative about clothing choices ('frumpy'). Negative words associated with behaviours focus on power and asserting a point of view ('ambitious', 'bossy', 'pushy' and 'bolshy').

Some words may not have fit so easily into these semantic fields. 'Shrill' and 'breathless' seem to refer to the sound of a woman's voice and 'working mum' refers to a woman's role – the terms used to describe these roles have been a focus of Chapter 2 but will also be relevant to Chapter 4 where we explore representation and identity.

Activity 2.2

If you completed a questionnaire to find out about people's current attitudes to gender and language use, you will have been contributing to your understanding of very specific features of language used to refer to men and women. If you explored your own language for attitudes and patterns of associations with gender you could revisit your findings after completeing Chapter 2. Practising a questionnaire will also prepare you for research methods that we will return to in Chapter 5.

Chapter 3

Activity 3.1

Metaphors centre on the sea, superheroes, fairy tales and famous books. In terms of equality, references to 'mermaids' versus 'pirates/sailors' represent women as 'other' – woman here are mythical beings, sometimes presented as tempters of men. In use with 'Neptune', Roman god of the sea, there is a power imbalance between the ordinary 'mermaids' and an all-powerful god. With 'ladies/fellas' there is an imbalance in the address terms used – the more traditional respectful term used for women and the more colloquial term used for men. References to fairy tales match a good, young and innocent female character ('Red Riding Hood') with their matching evil one ('Big Bad Wolf'). In the final literary reference to *The Great Gatsby*, the compound noun 'Dollfaces' stresses women's appearance in contrast to 'Old Sports' that references men's sense of fair play in competition and sport.

Activity 3.2

Alec's masculinity is presented through his control over both the horse and over Tess. His agency is shown through Hardy's positioning of Alec as the subject of most sentences: for example as in 'he loosened rein' and 'he drew rein where, in each one, he controls the horse's movements. Alec's ultimate exertion of physical power over Tess is highlighted in the declarative 'he gave her the kiss of mastery'; here the abstract noun 'mastery' foregrounds his male dominance. It is interesting that Tess is even compared to 'a wild animal, which suggests that Tess can be tamed by Alec.

In contrast, Tess's femininity is presented through actions that suggest her powerlessness, seen in the verbs 'trembling' and 'implored' alongside the metaphorical description of her as 'flushed with shame'. Tess is also depicted stereotypically as emotional, as in the noun phrase 'a big tear' and the reference to her 'attempts not to cry'. It becomes clear that Tess's attractiveness has made her an object for others to exploit. This is evident in the use of the passive voice to present Tess as like a doll being dressed 'up so prettily' by her mother, with the implication that this is a deliberate tactic to make her appealing to the rich Alec.

Alec's direct speech contains imperatives 'put your' and 'let me' and repeating the adverb 'now' shows his impatience. He uses different modes of address to convince Tess to accept his kisses, such as romantic and flattering terms like 'my beauty' and 'dear Tess' and another more metaphorical one 'you young witch' that presents him as helpless to resist her.

Activity 3.3

John is *nominated* by his first name. He is *functionalised* as a physician – a now more archaic term for a doctor – and *classified* by the reference to him being 'of high standing'. He is *relationally identified* by the narrator in a slightly distant way as 'one's own husband'. This is repeated with her brother, who the narrator says holds the same role and reputation.

In this extract from near the beginning of the story, it is clear that the actor with agency is John and he is activated throughout this passage. Relational verb

Ideas and answers

processes represent John as dominant and in control. The declaratives and syntax foreground John as the subject of the clause: 'John is practical', 'He has no patience with faith' and 'John is a physician'. The creation of male power and control is also re-emphasised when the narrator talks of her brother, further presenting her as a passivated actor in the decisions of the male family members. The narrator's passivated role is shown syntactically in the extract with her as the object: 'John laughs at me', but other language choices such as the repetition of the pronoun 'one', the interrogative 'what is one to do?' and exclamative 'you see he does not believe I am sick!' where her powerlessness is embedded within John's belief clause as he uses the negator 'not'; this creates the sense of her being acted upon and unable to stop their restrictions on her decision-making. At the end of the extract, the behavioural verb processes 'believe' and 'disagree' are modified by the adverb 'personally', but this too shows her passivated role as her own desires are unable to challenge the powerful male group of doctors and family members. Modality is also significant in the narrator's passivation: the adverb 'perhaps' and modal auxiliary verbs 'would not say it to a living soul', 'would do me good' and 'what can one do?' indicate her lack of certainty and commitment to her own feelings, emphasising the impossibility of the narrator asserting her own will against these powerful male forces.

Activity 3.4

The male social actors are called 'dads', 'stay-at-home fathers/dad', 'a house husband' or are nominated by a combination of their first and last names – 'Jackson Jones' and 'Richard Leigh'. In the first headline, grammatically they are made objects of actions through the passive voice: 'get bullied and are made to feel inadequate'. Interestingly this is by the social actors 'yummy mummies', a collocation associated with physically attractive and desirable women who are mothers. The pun 'man-cession' implies these men who stay at home are opting out of the workplace and their loss of desirability is a theme through the headlines. Look at the direct address to women: 'you can never fancy a man who becomes a house husband'. There are lots of references to loss in the headlines – in more abstract ways through the nouns 'dignity' and 'respect', and in financial terms as men who stay at home are presented as unable to manage money any more. A sense of men as damaging their wives' and children's lives also comes through in the language with verbs like 'fears' and 'harmed'.

Practice question

Discourse for women presents being a working mother as damaging and focuses on the effects on the children, specifically in terms of health, education and future life chances. For men, the implications of staying at home centre on the loss of professional, financial and sexual status, with this affecting the feelings that other family members have towards them. Both the discourses represent negatively men and women who do not adopt more traditional roles, suggesting a conservative one still exists. The discourses do not compete with each other but offer alternative ones from the accepted discourse of parenting roles and work. You might have analysed verbs as important both to the representation and overall message of the discourse; verbs contain much of the meaning (like 'struggles' for men, 'damage' for women) but also the use of the past tense for the men's headlines compares a successful past life in the workforce to their unsatisfactory life now in the home.

Chapter 4

Activity 4.1

You have explored your own identities and the ways that you present yourself to your family, friends and the other people that you are networked with through surveying your online accounts: Twitter, Facebook, Instagram, Snapchat and any blogs or forums you contribute to. What you 'like' or 'post' and the pictures that you upload probably represent many facets of yourself – your age, social background, experiences, culture and (of course) the ways that you want to present your sense of your own gender to others.

Activity 4.2

The teacher uses quite a few of the features that Lakoff highlights as typical of women's language. She hedges ('kinda') and uses negative politeness strategies in order not to impose on her peers' time and freedom of action, with conditionals like 'if you wanted to' and declaratives such as 'you don't have to do that'. If not quite tag questions, she uses back-channelling features, as in 'with all the ideas um you know' that seek some kind of support from her listeners. She also uses direct quotations when she reads from the script she has been given to introduce the roles. Throughout she uses qualifiers such as 'I think' and 'we're just' and modal constructions are also a key feature of her talk (for example, 'it wouldn't necessarily be').

What's interesting is how the speaker seemingly conforms to many of Lakoff's theories about the nature of women's language, despite social changes since the 1970s and more women in the workplace at a senior level. Indeed, she seems hesitant and uncertain in her new role and appears concerned at how this may impact on her departmental colleagues. She constantly tries to minimise this, presenting her own new identity in supporting teaching and learning in quite a passive way.

For Pamela Fishman, also in the dominance approach, this is a sign of 'conversational insecurity'. It is also important to note that this interaction has been taken out of its context and the assumption made about the speaker here might not be so relevant to her role as a teacher, where she may present a different identity to her students than her co-workers, showing that there can be localised and individual presentations of an apparent gendered identity that should not be generalised to all women.

Activity 4.3

In the adverts, other identities (age, ethnicity, cultural interests, occupation) all interact with gender.

Ideas and answers

Here's how you might have grouped the adjectives:

Adjectives used by women about themselves	Adjectives used by men about themselves
Appearance-related: *beautiful, blonde, brunette, attractive, good-looking, tall, fit, intelligent, elegant* Attributes: *professional, brave*	Appearance-related: *tall, slim, medium build* Attributes: *charming, considerate, unassuming, (can appear) interesting*
Adjectives used by women to describe ideal man	**Adjectives used by men to describe ideal woman**
Appearance-related: *tall, handsome, good-looking* Attributes: *professional, successful, kind, sweet-natured, warm, witty, loyal, open considerate*	Appearance-related: *feminine, slim, petite* Attributes: *friendly, happy-go-lucky, smiley*

Men seem to construct their masculine identities around height and build and attributes that they think might appeal to women. However, most of the male text producers described their interests rather than themselves. There were references to 'various creative and active interests', having a 'good state of health' and cultural references to music ('Pink Floyd Fan', 'John Lennon' and 'Elvis') and places ('Costa Blanca' and 'Barcelona').

For women, their representation of their feminine identities was very much through their appearance with references to hair colour and level of attractiveness – as if they think this is important to a man, In contrast, men seem more interested in a woman's size and shape and their level of friendliness. Women, more than men, appear to 'perform' gender in these personal adverts. The qualities that women seek from men are more behavioural than appearance-related – looking for a sense of humour and kindness. In one of the adverts, the male writer demonstrates their sense of humour with such comments as '44, only looks 43', rather than specifying or listing their own personal qualities.

Chapter 5

Activity 5.1

Hopefully, these steps helped you with your starting point for your research project and pinpointed the areas that interested you the most. If you didn't say yes to the topic areas suggested, you might have identified others that we haven't considered here. Noting down the types of texts and data that we have explored will have shown you the range of genres available to you, in addition to the methods and 'tools' used to research gender.

Language and Gender

Activity 5.2

Your task was to identify patterns and draw conclusions about the differences in collocations occurring with *man* and *woman* from the word sketch. What you may have found interesting is that the strongest collocates for *woman* were based around marital status (*widow, married, single, unmarried*) and age (*girl, child* and *youth*). For *man*, there was more of a range but some associations with power (*officer, god* and *world*) as well as explicit links to being an important part of the world (*nature* and *animal*).

Activity 5.3

Using the links to the websites and blogs should have allowed you to search for gender-related topics. These will have introduced you to different sources of information and views about gender, particularly more contemporary views. From reading some of the blogs and articles, you can see how gender as a topic of language study is of interest to wider audiences than just linguists. Indeed, it might also have shown you how linguistic topics can be of interest to the general public and how linguistic research can be packaged for a non-specialist audience in a very interesting and engaging way.

Practising Harvard referencing and using online referencing tools will be an invaluable skill to you as a student. There are many university websites that offer guidance, so although it can be initially daunting, there is a method for referencing any type of text you come across in your wider reading.

Practice question

Exploring the 'difference' approach might be a useful starting point for analysis with a hypothesis based on this. These texts are all written by young adults and age, as well as gender, could be a factor in their language choices. There appear more non-standard lexical and grammatical features in the texts written by males. They are also shorter than those written by the females. Technical jargon appears in both but the male texters discuss the effects of their training, whereas the female texters talk more generally about what activities they will do at the gym. Graphologically, the female texters use more emojis and kisses. In contrast, the male texters use more elliptical sentences and abbreviate words.

Transcription key

(.)	indicates a pause of less than a second
(2)	indicates a longer pause (number of seconds indicated)
Bold	indicates stressed syllables or words
: :	indicates elongation of a word
((*italics*))	indicates contextual or additional information
[ ]	indicates the start and end points of simultaneous speech

References

Austin, J. L. (1962) *How to Do Things with Words*. Oxford: Clarendon.

Baker, P. (2006) *Using Corpora for Discourse Analysis*. London: Continuum.

Baron-Cohen, S. (2003) *The Essential Difference: Men, Women and the Extreme Male Brain*. New York: Basic Books.

Baxter, J. (2014) *Double-voicing at Work: Power, Gender and Linguistic Expertise*. Palgrave Macmillan, London, p. 3.

Bornstein, K. (1998) *My Gender Workbook: How to Become a Real Man, a Real Woman, the Real You, or Something Else Entirely*. New York: Routledge.

Butler, J. (1990) *Gender Trouble: Feminism and the Subversion of Identity*. New York: Routledge.

Butler, J. (1993) *Bodies that Matter*. New York: Routledge.

Cambridge University Press (2016) *Language, Gender and Sport*. Cambridge: Cambridge University Press.

Cameron, D. (1995) *Verbal Hygiene*. London: Routledge.

Cameron, D. (2007) 'What Language Barrier?' *The Guardian* [online]. Available at: https://www.theguardian.com/world/2007/oct/01/gender.books [Accessed 23 August 2017].

Cheshire, J. (1982) 'Linguistic variation and social functions'. In S. Romaine (ed.) *Sociolinguistic Variation in Speech Communities*. London: Edward Arnold, pp. 153–66.

Connell, R.W. (1987) 'Hegemonic masculinity'. In S. Jackson and S. Scott (eds) (2002) *Gender: A Sociological Reader*. London: Routledge.

Connell, R. (2005) *Masculinities* (Second edition). Cambridge: Polity Press.

Eckert, P. and McConnell-Ginet, S. (1992) 'Think practically and look locally: language and gender as community-based practice'. *Annual Review of Anthropology* 21, pp. 461–90.

Fishman, P.M. (1978) 'Interaction: the work women do', *Social Problems* Vol. 25, pp. 397–406.

Foucault, M. (1972) *The Archaeology of Knowledge and the Discourse on Language*. New York: Pantheon.

Holmes, J. (1994) *Learning about Language: An Introduction to Sociolinguistics*. London: Longman.

Jespersen, O. (1922) *Language: Its Nature, Development and Origin*. London: G. Allen and Unwin.

Labov, W. (1966) *The Social Stratification of English in New York City*. Washington, DC: Center for Applied Linguistics.

References

Labov, W. (1972) 'The study of language in its social context', in Pier Paolo Giglioli (ed.), *Language and Social Context*. Harmondsworth: Penguin, pp. 283–307.

Labov, W. (2001) *Principles of Linguistic Change, Volume II: Social Factors*. Oxford: Wiley Blackwell.

Lakoff, G. and Johnson, M. (1980) *Metaphors We Live By*. Chicago: University of Chicago Press.

Lakoff, R. (1975) *Language and Woman's Place*. New York: Harper and Row.

Lave, J. and Wenger, E. (1991) *Situated Learning: Legitimate Peripheral Participation*. Cambridge: Cambridge University Press.

McWhorter, J. (2015) 'Goodbye to "he" and "she" and hello to "ze"?' CNN. Available at: http://edition.cnn.com/2015/10/14/opinions/mcwhorter-pronouns-gender-neutral/index.html [Accessed 23 August 2017]

Milroy, L. (1980) *Language and Social Networks*. Oxford: Blackwell.

Milroy, L. (1987) *Language and Social Networks* (Second edition). Oxford: Blackwell.

Searle, J.R. (1969) *Speech Acts: A lesson in the Philosophy of Language*. Cambridge: Cambridge University Press.

Sanghani, R. (2017) 'Feisty, frigid and frumpy: 25 words we only use to describe women'. *The Daily Telegraph* [online]. Available at: http://www.telegraph.co.uk/women/life/ambitious-frigid-and-frumpy-25-words-we-only-use-to-describe-wom/ [Accessed 23 August 2017].

Spender, D. (1980) *Man Made Language*. London: Routledge.

Sunderland, J. (2004) *Gendered Discourses*. Basingstoke: Palgrave Macmillan.

Tannen, D. (1990) *You Just Don't Understand: Men and Women in Conversation*. London: Virago.

Trudgill, P. (1972) 'Sex, covert prestige and linguistic change on the urban British English of East Anglia', *Language in Society* 1, pp. 179–95.

Van Leeuwen, T. (1996) 'The representation of social actors'. In C.R. Caldas-Coulthard and M. Coulthard (eds) *Texts and Practices: Readings in Critical Discourse Analysis*. London: Routledge.

Wenger, E. (1998) *Communities of Practice: Learning, Meaning and Identity*. Cambridge, Cambridge University Press.

Zimmerman, D. and West, C. (1975) Sex roles, interruptions and silences in conversation'. In B. Thorne, and N. Henley (eds) *Language and Sex: Difference and Dominance*. Rowley, Massachusetts: Newbury House, pp. 105–29.

Glossary

activation: where the social actor is the active forceful element in an activity

adjacency pairs: a simple structure of two turns

agency: (p. 80) a semantic concept where the agent (the doer of the action) is connected to the action expressed through the verb

agency: (p. 56) the one who is doing, often identified by the grammatical agent as the subject

anticipatory double-voicing: where the double-voicing anticipates and dilutes the criticism of others

argumentation theory: the study of how conclusions can be reached through logical reasoning

asymmetry: a power imbalance between speakers shown by the unequal way they address each other

binary oppositions: a pair of related terms that are opposite in meaning

blend: a word formed from two or more parts of other already existing words

blended mode: a text which contains conventional elements of both speech and writing

clipping: the process of shortening words by not articulating some of the sounds, usually at the beginning or ends of words

cognitive linguistics: the study of language that draws on insights from cognitive science

coinage: the invention of a new word or phrase

collocation: a word or phrase that is usually combined together with a greater frequency than chance

communities of practice: a group of people who come together for the purpose of a shared activity

compounding: the process of word formation that joins together two or more existing words to make a new word

conceptual metaphor: a structure that presents one concept in terms of another

connotation: the aura of emotional meaning that we associate with a word

Conversation Analysis (CA): an approach to the study of conversation in everyday interactions

corpora: a large collection of data usually stored electronically

corpus: a collection of texts brought together with the purpose of study

corpus linguistics: the study of language based on real-life examples collected together within a corpus

covert prestige: the status and prestige gained from using a non-standard variety of English

Glossary

Critical Discourse Analysis (CDA): an approach to studying language that focuses on aspects of social power and inequality in text and talk

deficit theory: the belief that the language used by women is inferior to that used by men

denotation: what a word stands for in its most literal sense

dialectology: the study of accents and dialects

difference theory of language: the belief that men and women have innate differences in the style and function of their speech and writing

discourse prosody: the ways that seemingly neutral words can be seen as having negative or positive associations through frequent use in collocations

discourses: combining meaning-making resources to present particular ways of seeing the world

dominance theory of language: the belief that the language differences between men and women can be explained by the hierarchical dominance of men in society

double-voicing: where speakers adjust their own language to reflect the agendas of the people with whom they are interacting

emphasised femininity: a complement to the hegemonic masculinity of men by accommodating the interests of men through feminine behaviours and attributes such as physical appearance

ethnographic research: the systematic study of groups of people and cultures carried out by close observation

euphemism: words or phrases that are substituted for more direct words or phrases in an attempt to make things easier to accept or less embarrassing

first-wave feminism: the movement that focused on getting the right for women to vote, to have property rights and the right to an education

folk linguistics: the opinions and beliefs that non-linguists hold about language use

gender neutral terms: words or phrases that avoid bias towards a particular gender

gender paradox: the phenomenon that women use more prestigious standard forms of English than men but that they also lead language change by adopting new forms of everyday English

genderlect: the particular dialect used by men and women according to their gender

grapheme: the smallest unit of the writing system such as the letter of the alphabet

hegemonic masculinity: behaviours and language associated with the idealised male group that is seen as having the most power and status in society

hold the conversational floor: speak until you have finished what you wish to say or until someone interrupts you

honorifics: a title or word expressing respect when used to address someone

hypercorrection: a pronunciation, word form or grammatical construction mistakenly perceived to be standard usage and substituted in a desire to be correct

hypothesis: a question or prediction used as a starting point for further investigation

ideological: relating to a system of ideas

interruption: the action of speaking at the same time as another speaker with the intention of taking the turn from them

joint negotiated enterprise: communities of practice share common goals and work together to achieve them

marked term: the unusual form of the term, often shown by an additional suffix

material verb process: verbs associated with actions and doing

mental verb process: verbs associated with thinking and feeling, or with perception

metaphor: a structure that presents one thing in terms of another

metonymy: references to things or concepts not by name but by something closely associated with them

mitigating double-voicing: where the double-voicing offsets the distance, reduces authority and builds solidarity with a team

mutual engagement: members of a community of practice come together in a common negotiated activity

nomination: the process of naming

noun phrase: a group of words built around a noun

observer's paradox: the issue of speakers being aware they are being recorded and the potential problems this may incur

overlaps: when one speaker talks at the same time as another

overt prestige: status gained by speakers from using a particular dialect or language

paralinguistic features: aspects of spoken language that do not involve words

passivation: where the social actor is the receiver of an action or event

patronymic: the element of a person's name that is based on the name of one's father, grandfather or other male ancestor

pejorative term: a judgemental term that usually implies disapproval or criticism

performatives: speech acts that explicitly perform an act, usually in a socially conventional situation such as a wedding ceremony, e.g. saying 'I do'.

performativity: the ability to use speech and other communication methods to construct or perform an identity

phonetician: a person who specialises in the study of sounds

political correctness: refers to the belief that language should not be used in a discriminatory way

post-modern feminism: the movement that covers different views and beliefs about women's rights and sees women as individuals as well as part of a group

Glossary

post-structuralist: a theory that rejects the notion of binary oppositions and sees that many perspectives exist rather than one fixed meaning

prescriptivism: the notion that language should be fixed, prescribing to a set standard of rules for language usage, with any shift away from these rules or standards being seen as incorrect

prosodic features: aspects of intonation, speed and volume

reclamation: the cultural process of removing negative associations with a particular term that has been used by a dominant group against a specific, less powerful social group

relational verb process: verbs associated with being, becoming or having

representation: the portrayal of events, people and circumstances through language and other meaning-making resources (e.g. images and sound) to create a way of seeing the world

second-wave feminism: the movement that focused on women's roles and rights within the workplace and in reproductive, sexuality and family issues

seed words: a list of words directly related to the topic that are used in the corpus search

semantic derogation: a process by which a word's meaning becomes more negative over time

semantic field: a group of words that fulfil the same kind of role and function in speech and writing

semantic shift: the changing of a word's meaning in a radically different way from its original use

semiology: the study of signs

shared repertoire: communities of practice share the same resources to communicate with each other and may have particular ways of doing or speaking

signified: the mental concept associated with the sign

signifier: the form which the sign takes, for example, a word or an image

simultaneous speech: where speakers talks at the same time as each other

Sketch Engine: a corpus tool to search language corpora

Social Actor Network: an analytical framework of categorising how social actors are represented

social constructivism: places the importance on social interaction as constructing identity and people coming together to form a shared construction of the world

social network theory: the study of how people in organisations and groups interact with each other

source domain: a concrete area of knowledge that is used to understand an abstract concept

speech act theory: the study of how words can be used to carry out actions

Standard English: a dialect of English considered 'correct' and 'normal', because it has distinctive and standardised features of spelling, vocabulary and syntax; it is the form of English usually used in formal writing

Language and Gender

stylistics: the study of texts both focusing carefully on language and providing a rich interpretation of key concerns, themes and possible effects

synchronous: interaction that takes place in real time

synonym: a word that has equivalent meaning to another word

tag question: a short question used at the end of a sentence, often inviting agreement with the speaker

target domain: the abstract concept/ area of knowledge that is understood in terms of a more concrete one

turn allocation: the process by which turns are managed in interactions

turn-taking: the process by which speakers co-construct conversation

turn transition relevance place: a point where it is natural for another speaker to take a turn

unmarked term: the regular or usual form of the term

uptalk: also known as high rising terminal, it refers to where declarative statements end with rising intonation

Valley Girl speak: the colloquial dialect associated with Californian English and the associated stereotype of girls who use this

variable: a contextual factor that can influence speech and writing

variational sociolinguistics: the study of the way that language changes in communities of speakers and the interaction between social factors and linguistic features

verb phrase: a group of words built around a head (main) verb

verbal verb process: verbs associated with saying and communicating

vocal fry: a vocal effect produced by the very slow vibration of the vocal cords and characterised by a creaking sound and low pitch

word sketch: a short corpus-created summary of a word's collocational behaviour that has been automatically generated

Word Sketch difference: an online search tool used to compare and contrast two words by analysing their collocations and by displaying the collocates divided into categories based on grammatical relations

Index

Page numbers in italics are figures; with 't' are tables.

acknowledgement of sources 94
argumentation theory 53–6

communities of practice 11, 12–13, 84
compounding 26–7
Conversation Analysis (CA) 89–91
corpus data 56–8, *57*
corpus linguistics 84–8
Critical Discourse Analysis (CDA) 44–5, 49, 84

data types for research 81–3, 88–9
decision-making 95–6
deficit approach 4–6
difference approach 10–11, 10t
discourse 38–9, 51–2
  and identity 62–4
diversity approach 11–13
dominance approach 9–10

ethics 89
ethnography 4–5, 83–4

feminism 3
food metaphors 32–3, 44

gender, defined 2, 19–20, 20t
generic terms 21–3

health magazines 52–3

identity 16, 28, 61
  and discourse 62–4
  and masculinities 64–7, *66*
  and occupational talk 69–71
  and phonology 67–9

social constructionism/constructivism 14–15, 62–4, 72–3, 73–4t
  and social media 74–6, *75*
inflections 24–6

literature 45–6

marking gender 23–8
masculinity, and identity 64–7
meaning 26–7, 39–43, *40–2*, 43t
media 47–8
  health magazines 52–3
  social 74–6, *75*, 92–3
metaphors 28–9, 31–3, 43–4

occupational talk 69–71
order, word 21–3

patterns 28–9
performance approach 14–16
phonology, and identity 67–9
political correctness 13–14, 24, 33–6, 33–4t
post-structuralist approach 72–4
power 44–6, 66–7
pronouns 33–4

questionnaires 82

reclamation of words 35–6
representation
  and argumentation theory 53–6
  corpus data 56–8, *57*
  and discourse 38–9, 51–2

and health magazines 52–3
  and metaphor 43–4
  and power 44–6
  and semiotics 39–43, *40–2*, 43t
  social actor 46–51
research 78–9
  acknowledgement of sources 94
  analysis 89–93
  creating a project 79–88, 80–1t, 86t, *88*
  decision-making 95–6
  secondary reading 93–4
  and spoken data 88–9

secondary reading 93–4
semiotics 39–43, *40–2*, 43t
Sketch Engine 85
social actor representation 46–51
social constructionism/constructivism 14–15, 62–4, 72–3, 73–4t
social media 74–6, *75*, 92–3
social networks 11, 12
stylistics 84

titles of address 27–8
toilet signs 41–3

uptalk 68

variationist approach 7–9
vocal fry 69

Word Sketch difference 85–7

Acknowledgments

The authors and publishers acknowledge the following sources of copyright material and are grateful for the permissions granted. While every effort has been made, it has not always been possible to identify the sources of all the material used, or to trace all copyright holders. If any omissions are brought to our notice, we will be happy to include the appropriate acknowledgements on reprinting.

Text 3D and 3E web-banners from Men's Health and Women's Health Magazine online, used with permission from Wright's Media.

Development of this publication has made use of the Cambridge English Corpus (CEC). The CEC is a multi-billion word computer database of contemporary spoken and written English. It includes British English, American English and other varieties of English. It also includes the Cambridge Learner Corpus, developed in collaboration with Cambridge English Language Assessment. Cambridge University Press has built up the CEC to provide evidence about language use that helps to produce better language teaching materials.

Thanks to the following for permission to reproduce images:

Cover image Sujata Jana/EyeEm/Getty Images; chapter opener images 1-5 H. Armstrong Roberts/ClassicStock/Getty Images, Alys Tomlinson/Getty Images, Jay Shaw Baker/NurPhoto via Getty Images, Sara D. Davis/Getty Images, Hero images/Getty Images; Figure 3.3 mrtom-uk/Getty Images

The publisher would like to thank the following members of The Cambridge Panel: English who assisted in reviewing this book: Stephanie Atkinson, Obadia Somelia and Mary Owuor.